THE PROMISED ONE

To John,
May God richly bless
you and your family!

Sally Berk

THE PROMISED ONE

ONE

THE MYSTERY OF THE MESSIAH

SALLY H. BERK

Life Springs Press
Aiken, SC

Maps were created with software from BibleMapper.com.

Cover design by James Steidl.
Interior design by Kendra Cagle.
eBook Conversion by Valerie Stuart.
Author photo by John Karasch.

Life Springs Press
P.O. Box 7152
Aiken, SC 29804
www.lifespringspress.com

ISBN: 978-0-9976966-0-8 (print version)
ISBN: 978-0-9976966-1-5 (electronic version)

And beginning with Moses and all the Prophets,
He interpreted to them in all the Scriptures the things concerning Himself.

—Luke 24:27

Table of Contents

From the Author

This study began as a personal quest to know more about God's promises and developed into a passion for the Old Testament and its portrayal of a uniquely loving, compassionate, and just God. It is my hope that *The Promised One* will inspire fresh appreciation for the good news of His unfailing love and grace, expressed throughout the Holy Scriptures.

Acknowledgements

I want to thank all who have encouraged me with their kind words and prayers, especially Judith Hartzell, Mona Ruse, Joyce Rechkemer, Louise Fritz, Delron Shirley, Amy Persons-Birch, Drew Kornreich, Robert Paul and Debbie Lamb, Rusty Smith, Kelli Sumter, Sue Mathley, and Eva Edl. Special thanks also to Professors Bryan E. Beyer and Larry Dixon for their helpful input.

Most of all, I want to thank my family: my daughter Mary, for her assistance with the maps and questions about technology; my daughter Sarah, for her editorial insights and patience in reading revisions; and my husband, John, who always encouraged me to keep doing what I loved.

Introduction

The Promised One: the Mystery of the Messiah takes readers on a guided journey through the books of Genesis and Exodus and examines the prophecies of the Messiah found in the Psalms and the books of the prophets. In each section, the designated Scripture passages are to be read first, followed by the accompanying text. Questions for reflection and discussion are included in each chapter, and an answer key is located at the end of the book.

Abbreviations

Bible Versions

AMP	*The Amplified Bible*
ESV	*English Standard Version*
JPS	*The Jewish Publication Society Hebrew-English Tanakh*
KJV	*King James Version*
NIV	*New International Version*
NKJV	*New King James Version*

CHAPTER 1
The Promise
(Genesis, chapters 1–4)

The opening chapters of Genesis describe God's creation of the heavens and the earth, His relationship with Adam and Eve, their rebellion, and His gracious promise to send a Rescuer. This account, attributed to Moses, lays the foundation for all that follows in the biblical narrative.

In the Beginning, God

Genesis 1:1

The Bible opens by introducing God, the universe, and a particular planet as the setting for the narrative. The Hebrew word for God in this verse is a plural noun, *Elohim*. Some read it as the "plural of majesty"; others see it as conveying the idea of one God but allowing for a "plurality of persons," as in the Trinity. [1]

God existed before the physical universe and spoke it into existence *ex nihilo*—out of nothing. [2]

> *By the word of the LORD the heavens were made, and by the breath of his mouth all their host...For he spoke, and it came to be; he commanded, and it stood firm.*
>
> *—Psalm 33:6, 9 (ESV)*

Genesis 1:2–5

The deep waters covering the earth lacked any form or differentiation. The Spirit of God hovered over them until, suddenly, God's voice split the silence and light exploded into existence.

God named the light and the darkness and separated them. Evening and morning constituted one day—a period of time.

Genesis 1:6–13

On the second and third days, God continued to speak new phenomena into existence, separate them in form and function, and name each one. [3]

On the second day, He created the expanse of Heaven, which separated the waters above from those below. On the third day, He caused dry land to appear and named it "Earth"; He called the waters "Seas." Having prepared the heavens and the earth, God then brought forth the first plants and trees, giving each one the ability to reproduce after its own kind.

Genesis 1:14–19

On the fourth day, God placed lights in the heavens and established their functions: to divide time into alternating intervals of day and night, to mark seasons and years, and to illuminate the earth.

> The verb "to create" (Hebrew, *bara'*) occurs in three places in Genesis 1 and emphasizes the creation of something entirely new: when God creates the heavens and the earth (Gen. 1:1); when He creates conscious life (Gen. 1:21); and when He creates human beings (Gen. 1:27). [4]

Genesis 1:20–23

God created the first conscious life on the fifth day in the form of sea creatures and winged fowl, each with the ability to reproduce after its own kind.

Genesis 1:24–31

On the sixth day, God caused the earth to bring forth both domestic and wild animals and creatures that move along the ground. Last of all, He created human beings "in His own image."

All human beings bear the stamp of God's image. For example, creativity, a love of order, and an appreciation for beauty are all part of God's nature. When we design and produce a useful object, undertake to organize a messy room, or admire a beautiful sunset, we give evidence that we are created in His likeness.

1. *What characteristics or personal qualities do you associate with the phrase "made in the image of God"?*

_____

_____

God blessed the first couple and charged them to be fruitful and multiply and to fill and subdue the earth.

> 2. *What additional responsibility did He assign them (v. 28)?*
>
> _____
>
> _____

All forms of conscious life were to sustain themselves by eating plants, not each other. God surveyed all His work and was pleased, calling it *very good.*

Genesis 2:1–3
The earth, once dark and without form, was now a showcase of light and life, beauty, variety, complexity, and order. All creation reflected the intelligence, power, and goodness of its Designer and Sustainer.

On the seventh day, God ceased to create and rested. In blessing the seventh day, He set it apart as holy. In Hebrew, the verb *shabat* (to rest) is the root of the word "Sabbath."[5]

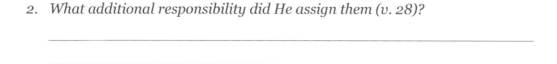

And God blessed the seventh day and made it holy, because on it he rested from all the work of creating that he had done.

—Genesis 2:3 (NIV)

Matchmaker

Chapter one provides the general setting and background for all that follows. In chapter two, the focus "zooms in" on a particular locale, and additional details are provided about the creation of the first human beings and their relationship with their Creator.

Genesis 2:4–15
God created the first man and designed a pleasant garden for him to tend. He placed a single restriction on Adam's freedom and attached a consequence—a curse—for violating it.

Genesis 2:16–17

3. *What was the curse?*

_____

_____

_____

_____

> *Adam*, the Hebrew word for man, is both a general term for humankind (Gen. 1:26–27) and the proper name of the first man. A related word, *adamah*, describes the reddish soil from which God created Adam. [6]

Each time Adam walked past one particular tree, he had to choose: pick the fruit and taste it, or obey God and walk on.

Genesis 2:18–25
God delegated to Adam the task of naming the land animals and birds, giving him complete freedom in the work.

In all creation, Adam was alone, having no one of his own kind to be with him. Then, from Adam's rib, God created a counterpart for him.

When Adam saw Eve, he affirmed that it was God's will for a man and a woman to form a lasting relationship, becoming "one flesh." Together, the first couple had all they needed to be happy and at peace in the Garden.

Intruder in the Garden

Genesis 3:1–6
The serpent chose to target Eve with his deception. She understood God's command not to eat the fruit of one particular tree and the consequence for disobedience. However, when the serpent told her that God had lied in order to withhold something beneficial from her, she did not immediately reject the idea. Instead, she began to turn it over in her mind.

4. *According to the serpent, why had God forbidden Eve to eat the fruit of the tree of life?*

_____

_____

Eve considered the possibilities. Would this particular fruit give her a new, higher kind of knowledge? Did God want to keep her from reaching her potential?

Adam, too, failed to reject the serpent's lie outright. Might the fruit benefit them rather than kill them? Could it be that God could not be trusted?

By eating the fruit, Adam and Eve committed high treason, rejecting God's sovereignty and aligning themselves with His adversary. Their disobedience is traditionally referred to as "the Fall."

A New Look

Genesis 3:7–10
After eating the fruit, Adam and Eve quickly became aware of a change in their physical appearance and hastily made coverings for their bodies. [7]

> 5. *When Adam and Eve heard God walking in the garden, what emotion did they experience for the first time?*

Adam could have answered God's question with a simple "Over here!" Instead, he confessed his fear and the reason for it.

Genesis 3:11–13
God "convened court" in the Garden and questioned Adam and Eve.

> 6. *How did Adam explain his disobedience?*

> 7. *How did Eve explain her disobedience?*

These "pass-the-buck" responses confirmed their now-fallen condition. Fear and guilt had replaced peace and harmony in their relationship with God and each other.

The Sentence—and a Promise

Genesis 3:14–15
God pronounced sentence first on the serpent, condemning it to exist in an altered physical form.

> 8. *How did God describe the future relationship between Eve and the serpent, and between her offspring and the serpent's offspring?*
>
> _____
>
> _____

God prophesied a state of war in which a Descendant of Eve would triumph over the serpent, crushing his head under His feet. In the battle, this promised Deliverer would be wounded in the heel.

God's promise of a Rescuer radically altered Adam and Eve's otherwise hopeless situation. Deserving judgment, they heard a promise of mercy. His next pronouncements, however, held no good news for either one.

Genesis 3:16–20
In addition to suffering pain in childbirth, Eve would experience a change in her relationship with her husband.[8] Adam would struggle to make a living in a natural environment gone awry. Rather than harvesting fruit from thriving trees (Gen. 2:16), he would labor to raise crops in weed-infested soil.

Neither Adam nor Eve expired immediately, but the process of death and dying had been set in motion for them and for all creation. And yet, Eve's name, meaning "life-spring," spoke of hope for the future.

Continuing Relationship

Genesis 3:21
Because of their disobedience, a just God could have abandoned Adam and Eve, leaving them to fend for themselves. Instead, He showed them mercy, graciously providing new coverings to replace their leafy garments. The coverings were evidence of His continuing love, but they came at a price—the lives of innocent animals.

> *I will greatly rejoice in the LORD, my soul shall exult in my God; for he has clothed me with the garments of salvation, he has covered me with the robe of righteousness.*
>
> *—Isaiah 61:10 (ESV)*

God did not permit Adam and Eve to linger in the Garden. He put them out and provided an angelic guard to protect the way to the tree of life.

9. *Why was it important for Adam and Eve not to eat from the tree of life at this time?*

_____

_____

Fallen human nature remains at the heart of most of the world's ills. Greed, envy, selfishness, and lust for power have marred and complicated human relationships ever since the Garden of Eden and continue to undermine even well-intentioned efforts to build just and happy societies.

Life Goes On

Genesis 4:1–2
After being expelled from the Garden, Adam and Eve began to fulfill their calling to "be fruitful and multiply" (Gen. 1:28).

10. *How did Eve indicate that she continued to enjoy a personal relationship with God?*

_____

_____

In raising their children, Adam and Eve taught them about their Creator, the Fall, and God's promise to send a Rescuer. Both Cain and Abel grew up hearing the truth, but only one continued to walk in its light, ordering his ways to please and honor God.

Offerings: What's Acceptable?

Genesis 4:3–5

The types of offerings brought by Cain and Abel expressed their differing attitudes toward God. In sacrificing firstborn lambs from his flock, Abel looked back to God's provision of coverings for his parents in the Garden.[9] Like Adam and Eve, he acknowledged his need for God's mercy and remembered His promise to send a Rescuer.

Cain, however, brought produce—the ripe fruits, grains, and vegetables he had toiled to raise. In doing so, he made himself judge of what constituted an acceptable sacrifice, saying, in effect, "Accept me on my own terms."

Genesis 4:6–7

11. *What did Cain need to do to be accepted?*

_____

_____

Genesis 4:8–16

Cain refused to heed God's counsel and went his own way. Subsequently, when he took his brother's life, he expressed no remorse.

Parting of the Ways

In the generations that followed, people chose either Cain's way or Abel's way of approaching God. Those who agreed with Cain believed that they could be accepted by God on the basis of their own efforts and on their own terms. Those who followed in the tradition of Abel continued to rely on God's mercy as they looked forward to the fulfillment of His promise to send a Rescuer.

Because God provided so few details about the Promised One, people could only speculate about His identity and mission:

Who would He be?
When and where would He appear?
How could He be recognized?
What would He do to defeat the enemy?

Notes:

CHAPTER 2

Abraham
(Genesis, chapters 5–23)

Genesis 5:1–11:26

As people multiplied on the earth, some, like Abel, trusted God and His promise of rescue; others, like Cain, devised new belief systems, ordering their lives and worship practices according to their own ideas.

Eventually, only one family of eight people remained faithful to God. When a worldwide flood covered even the highest mountaintops, only those eight survived, along with the creatures they brought with them into the ark.

When the floodwaters receded and the ark came to rest on land, Noah and his family began life anew in a vastly altered environment. At first, they and their descendants continued to worship the Almighty, acknowledging their dependence upon Him. As time passed, however, some again rebelled. Refusing to acknowledge God as Creator, they developed alternate explanations for reality. By 2100 B.C., these alternative worldviews dominated the cultures of Mesopotamia, Canaan, and Egypt, and those who held to the truth were once again greatly outnumbered. [1]

About this time, God set in motion His plan to establish an alliance with a special nation—a unique people who would voluntarily commit themselves to walk in His ways and await the coming of the Promised One.

The Instrument

Throughout the ancient Near East, powerful kings forged alliances with weaker, neighboring rulers by means of legal instruments known as *suzerainty treaties*. In these contracts, or covenants, the mighty ruler, or suzerain, offered to protect and promote the interests of a vassal-king in exchange for his oath of loyalty and obedience. Typically, "obedience" involved paying tribute, acting as an enemy to the suzerain's enemies, and providing troops upon request. [2]

Once finalized, a suzerainty treaty created a type of family relationship. In written correspondence, a suzerain addressed his vassal as both "son" and "servant," and a vassal called his suzerain "father" as well as "lord." A vassal "loved" his suzerain by trusting his benevolence at all times and keeping the terms of the contract. [3]

The Invitation

Genesis 11:27–12:6
When God spoke to Abram in Haran, He proposed a type of suzerainty treaty. The benefits He offered, however, went far beyond what any earthly suzerain could provide:

> *And I will make of you a great nation, and*
> *I will bless you, and make your name great, so that you will be a blessing.*
> *I will bless those who bless you and him who dishonors you, I will curse, and*
> *in you all the families of the earth shall be blessed.*
>
> *—Genesis 12:1–3 (ESV)*

1. *The blessings were conditional upon Abram's obedience. What did God require him to do?*

_____

_____

With God's promises as his only security, Abram set out for Canaan, accompanied by Sarai, his wife, and Lot, his nephew, in a slow-moving caravan. His departure marked the beginning of a relationship with God that was to benefit not only him and his household but, in time, all peoples of the earth. [4]

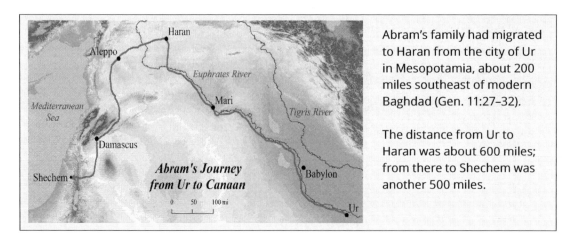

Abram's family had migrated to Haran from the city of Ur in Mesopotamia, about 200 miles southeast of modern Baghdad (Gen. 11:27–32).

The distance from Ur to Haran was about 600 miles; from there to Shechem was another 500 miles.

Abram's caravan entered Canaan and arrived at the city of Shechem, located in a valley between two mountains, about forty miles north of present-day Jerusalem.

Genesis 12:7–8
In Shechem, God appeared to Abram and promised to give his descendants the very land on which he stood.

> 2. *How did Abram respond when he heard this promise?*

Moving on, Abram built a second altar and called on the name of the Lord (Hebrew, *YHWH*), then continued to journey southward.

The two altars remained as markers in the land, testifying to Abram's loyalty to *Yahweh* and trust in His promises.

> "Abram called on the name of the Lord" (Gen. 12:8). In many English Bibles, "Lord" is substituted for the Hebrew *YHWH*, often translated as *"Yahweh."*[5] According to Genesis 4:26, people began to call upon God by His name *Yahweh* after Seth was born to Adam and Eve.

Opportunities

In courting a prospective vassal, a suzerain bestowed gifts and other forms of benevolence known as "kindnesses," and he watched for evidence that the lesser king would prove loyal and obey the terms of a treaty, or covenant, once it was ratified. At the same time, the prospective vassal-king could observe and assess the character of the suzerain.

In the days and years ahead, God would prove His goodness and faithfulness multiple times to His prospective vassal, and Abram would have more than one opportunity to demonstrate his trustworthiness to his divine Suzerain.

Opportunity #1: Life in Danger?

Genesis 12:9–13:2
Leaving Bethel, Abram traveled in a southerly direction. When a famine hit Canaan, he continued on to Egypt. Along the way, he began to fear that an Egyptian official, upon seeing Sarai's extraordinary beauty, might abduct her and murder him. Instead of relying on God to protect him, Abram asked Sarai to lie about her identity and did not protest when she was taken into Pharaoh's harem.

3. How did God subsequently discipline Abram for his lack of faith and failure to protect Sarai?

_____

Thanks to God's mercy and faithfulness, Sarai was delivered, and Abram departed from Egypt with his life intact and with great wealth.

Altar at Tel Arad, Israel.
©Hanan Isachar/hanan-isachar
photography.com.

Genesis 13:3–4
Having returned to the altar at Bethel, a grateful Abram called once more on the name of *Yahweh.*

4. When people call on God, they usually have a specific purpose in mind—to worship, ask forgiveness, express appreciation, make a request, or perhaps remind Him of a promise. What might have been Abram's purpose in calling on God at this time?

_____

_____

> *The Lord is near to all who call upon Him, to all who call upon Him sincerely and in truth.*
>
> *—Psalm 145:18 (AMP)*

Opportunity #2: Do You See What I See?

Genesis 13:5–13
Abram's growing prosperity had one downside: he now had so many herds and flocks that his shepherds and Lot's were competing for pasture. When Abram gave Lot the choice of where to live, he opted for the well-watered Jordan Valley.

5. *What did Abram's invitation to Lot indicate about his trust in God's faithfulness?*

_____

_____

With Lot's departure, Abram was alone in the land, separated from all his relatives (Gen. 12:1).

Genesis 13:14–18

God spoke to Abram, reaffirming His promises of land and many descendants. He directed Abram to look out in all directions and walk through the land where his descendants would one day live and become as numerous as "the dust of the earth."

Abram settled in Hebron, where he built another altar—a third landmark in the region.

Opportunity #3: Caution—Strings Attached!

Genesis 14:1–16

King Chedolaomer, in alliance with three other kings, defeated five Canaanite rulers who had rebelled against him. When the fighting was over, Abram's nephew, Lot, was a prisoner of war.

Acting as kinsman-redeemer, Abram pursued his nephew's captors far into modern-day Syria. The fact that he could muster 318 armed men, all born in his household, was evidence of his great prosperity.

> A kinsman-redeemer (Hebrew, *goel*) is one who uses his wealth and/or position to benefit a close relative in difficult or unjust circumstances. [6]

Genesis 14:17–24

Melchizedek, a king and priest, gave glory to God for Abram's victory; [7] the king of Sodom, on the other hand, sought to recoup honor for himself after his defeat by King Chedolaomer.

6. *When invoking a blessing on Abram, what name and title for God did Melchizedek use?*

_____

_____

7. *To what deity had Abram made a vow?*

_____

_____

The priest-king Melchizedek and Abram both worshiped the Most High God, the Possessor of heaven and earth. No such common ground linked Abram and Bera, the king of Sodom. [8]

King Bera was indebted to Abram for retrieving his subjects and their property. In an effort to regain the position of power-broker, he offered Abram a gift of spoils. If Abram had accepted, he would have been indebted to Bera and, by extension, to his gods. Abram refused to give the king of Sodom any grounds for claiming to be his benefactor. [9]

By refusing the offer of spoils, Abram proved that his loyalty was to God alone, and his faithfulness was soon rewarded.

Decision Time

> *Fear not, Abram: I AM thy shield and thy reward shall be exceedingly great.*
>
> *—Genesis 15:1 (KJV)*

Genesis 15:1–7
God spoke to Abram in a vision and initiated the first of two steps in a covenant enactment.

God identified Himself as Abram's "shield"—i.e., his protector and benefactor; [10] in his reply, Abram addressed God for the first time by the title *Adonai* (Lord). [11]

To Abram, the word "reward" (v. 1) implied a benefit due as part of their agreement, and he spoke to God in the manner of a servant asking his master about a promise not yet kept. [12]

8. *How did God respond to Abram's complaint?*

_____

_____

Looking up at the starry night sky, Abram believed God's promise of an heir and entrusted his future wholly to Him. In that moment, he accepted unconditionally the role of vassal-prince of the Most High God. [13]

> *He determines the number of the stars and calls them each by name.*
>
> *—Psalm 147:4 (NIV)*

9. *How did God respond to Abram's faith?*

_____

_____

This exchange constituted a legal transaction—a virtual "signing on the dotted line." God's gift of righteousness elevated Abram from "prospective" to "accepted" covenant partner.

To conclude the transaction, God repeated His name and His promise to give Abram the land as an inheritance.

> This step was similar in significance to a betrothal in an ancient Jewish marriage contract. A betrothed couple was considered legally married but did not share all the benefits of the union until after the wedding ceremony. [14]

A Guarantee

Genesis 15:8–16

When Abram, conscious of his new standing, boldly asked for a guarantee of the land-grant, God instructed him to make preparations for the swearing of an oath.

In Abram's time, one accepted way to solemnize an oath called for the individual to sacrifice an animal, split its carcass into two sections, and walk between them while invoking a curse—i.e., calling on his gods to make him like the dead animal if he failed to keep his promise. The practice was known as "cutting a covenant" or "cutting a treaty." [15]

10. *In his dream, what did Abram see passing between the halves of the slain animals?*

_____

_____

Genesis 15:17–21

The cloud of smoke and the blazing torch indicated God's Presence passing between the carcasses. [16] Thus, the Creator of heaven and earth swore to keep His promise—or become like the slain animals. God's grant of land was as certain as His very existence!

Having received the guarantee of land, Abram could now look forward to final ratification of the treaty. He could do nothing, however, to bring this event about; it would take place in God's timing.

Time Flies

Genesis 16:1–16

God had promised Abram a son, but He had not yet specified that Sarai would be the mother. When she suggested an alternate, culturally acceptable way to have a family, Abram was open to the idea. "After all," he may have reasoned, "wouldn't God want us to use every means available to obtain the promised heir?"

Abram's union with Hagar produced Ishmael, and for the next thirteen years, he and Sarai acted on the assumption that Ishmael was the heir God had promised.

Final Step

Genesis 17:1–8

Abram was ninety-nine years old when God again appeared to him and, identifying Himself as *El Shaddai* (Almighty God), announced His intention to ratify His covenant. If Abram would agree to walk in God's ways, then He would finalize the treaty. This condition was non-negotiable: Abram would enjoy the covenant benefits only if he conducted his affairs according to God's will.

> 11. *How did Abram indicate his consent?*
>
> ---
>
> ---

Next, God repeated His promise to make Abram the father of many nations and gave him a new name: "Abram" means "exalted father"; "Abraham" means "father of a multitude." [17]

At this point, God's title also changed; He became, officially, "the God of Abraham."

Each of the covenant blessings God pronounced on Abraham concerned not only Abraham but also his posterity:

> *I will make you exceedingly fruitful, and*
> *I will make you into nations, and kings shall come from you.*
>
> *And I will establish my covenant between me and you and your offspring after*
> *you throughout their generations for an everlasting covenant,*
> *to be a God to you and to your offspring after you.*
>
> *And I will give to you and to your offspring the land of your sojournings,*
> *all the land of Canaan, for an everlasting possession,*
>
> *And I will be their God.*
>
> *—Genesis 17:6–8 (ESV)*

Genesis 17:9–14

In the ancient Near East, cutting a covenant often involved an animal sacrifice.[18] However, God directed Abraham to finalize his commitment in a different way: He commanded him and all those under his authority to be circumcised.

Carried out in connection with the covenant, circumcision implied a curse: "If I am unfaithful to my vow, may God cut me off like the discarded foreskin." By being circumcised, Abraham would commit himself to serve *Yahweh* as a loyal and obedient vassal. [19]

From then on, circumcision was to be the sign, or memorial, of God's covenant with Abraham.

Genesis 17:15–21

To signify Sarai's inclusion in the covenant, God changed her name also. Both "Sarai" and "Sarah" designate a person of authority; "Sarah" connotes royalty—a noble lady, princess, or queen.[20]

God knew the thoughts that went through Abraham's mind upon hearing that Sarah was to conceive a son—thoughts of age and physical limitations—and assured him that a son named Isaac would one day inherit the promises and take his father's place as God's covenant partner.

For over a decade, Abraham had looked on Ishmael, his son by Hagar, as his heir. According to the conventions of the time, however, once a son was born to Sarah, Ishmael would lose his inheritance rights. [21]

Abraham's joy quickly turned to concern as he grasped the consequences for Ishmael. How, he wondered, did Ishmael fit into God's plan now? What was to become of this son whom he dearly loved?

12. How did God comfort Abraham regarding Ishmael?

_____

_____

Ishmael would be blessed and would become a mighty nation, but God's special covenant promises would belong to Isaac alone.

Genesis 17:23–27
Without delay, Abraham, along with all the males in his household, carried out God's command to be circumcised.

Genesis 18:1–8
By accepting Abraham's invitation and partaking of the feast he prepared, *El Shaddai* celebrated the new family relationship.

Genesis 18:9–15
Apparently, Abraham had not yet shared with Sarah what God had revealed to him—that at the age of ninety she was to conceive a child.

Family Privileges

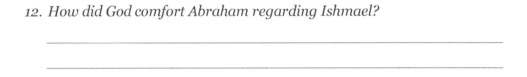

Shall I hide from Abraham [My friend and servant] what I am going to do?

—Genesis 18:17 (AMP)

Genesis 18:16–19

Having been granted full standing as covenant partner of *Yahweh*, Abraham soon found himself enjoying a new privilege: participation in a royal council.

Before revealing His plans to Abraham, God explained His reasons for doing so. First, He cited two of the promises He had made to His vassal-prince:

> 13. *Abraham would become:*
>   *a)* _____ *, and*
>   *b)* _____*would be blessed in him.*

Then, God reminded Abraham of his responsibility to teach his children and his household to walk in God's ways.

Genesis 18:20–33

In sharing His intention to judge Sodom, God treated Abraham as a trusted friend or family member whose input He valued. Abraham seized the opportunity and boldly sought to persuade God to spare the city.

> 14. *To what aspect of God's character did Abraham appeal?*
>
> _____

Genesis 19:1–29

The next morning, Abraham returned to the very location where he had interceded for Lot and viewed the still-smoking wasteland that had once been Sodom and Gomorrah. He had no way of knowing that, in the midst of judgment, God had shown mercy to Lot and his family.

> *All the paths of the Lord are mercy and steadfast love, even truth and faithfulness are they for those who keep His covenant and His testimonies.*
>
> *—Psalm 25:10 (AMP)*

Birth Announcement

Genesis 20:1-18

In Gerar, Abraham once again asked Sarah to lie to protect him, and, once again, God graciously rescued her and blessed him. The silver that King Abimelech weighed out to vindicate Sarah was five hundred times the price of a slave. [22]

> 15. *In addition to bestowing lavish gifts, how did Abimelech show his new respect for Abraham, the servant-prince of Yahweh (v. 15)?*

_____

_____

Genesis 21:1–8

Sarah had once laughed upon hearing God's prophecy that she was to bear a son (Gen. 18:12); now, she laughed out of pure joy at its fulfillment.

Genesis 21:9–21

As Abraham struggled to obey God and send Ishmael away, God again assured him He would watch over and preserve this son also.

A Wise King

Genesis 21:22–34

Even though Abraham was still a transient who owned no property and had no legal standing in any city-state of Canaan, King Abimelech sought a nonaggression pact with him. The fact that both Abraham and Abimelech swore an oath (v. 31) indicated that it was a parity treaty—a covenant between equals. Both men expected it to be binding also upon their descendants (v. 23). [23]

At this time, Abraham and Abimelech settled a dispute over ownership of a well, and the location became known as *Beersheba* (Well of the Oath). The tamarisk tree Abraham planted may have served as a lasting memorial of the covenant.

Tamarisk tree at Tel Hasi, Israel.
©Hanan Isachar/Isachar-photography.com

Obedient Servant

Sending Ishmael away had been an immensely difficult trial for Abraham. What God asked him to do next, however, tested the very limits of his faith.

Abraham acknowledged God's right as Suzerain to ask anything of his servant, and he understood that it was his duty as vassal-prince always to trust his Suzerain's goodness. But, how could he offer his beloved Isaac as a sacrifice—the son whom God had promised and who was to inherit the covenant blessings?

Genesis 22:1–8
As Abraham set out for the mountains, every step brought him closer to the defining moment: would he keep his covenant obligation?

If he obeyed God, there would be only one hope for his son's survival: that God would keep His promises concerning Isaac (Gen. 17:19, 21; 21:12).

> In Genesis 22:2, God speaks of Isaac as Abraham's only son. The Hebrew word translated "only" indicates "united." Abraham and his beloved son Isaac were united in God's covenant purposes. [24]

16. *In speaking to his servants, how did Abraham express his trust in God's faithfulness?*

_____

_____

In responding to Isaac's question, Abraham again voiced his trust in God.

Genesis 22:9–14
Having reached his destination, Abraham prepared to obey God. He placed Isaac on the altar and lifted the knife, believing God would keep His promises, even if He had to raise Isaac from the dead.

At the last possible moment, God arrested Abraham's upraised arm and provided a ram for him to offer instead of Isaac.

Genesis 22:15–18

Abraham's trust and obedience brought immense joy to God. Exulting, God vowed a second time to perform for His trustworthy partner and friend all that He had promised. The Almighty swore by Himself (v. 16)—i.e., called upon Himself to witness and enforce the oath—because no higher authority exists.

Property Owner at Last

Genesis 23:1–6

More than three decades later, Abraham still owned no property in Canaan; consequently, when Sarah died, he had no place to bury her.

In the eyes of his Hittite neighbors, Abraham was a foreigner who kept himself separate and did not worship their gods. At first, these friends seemed reluctant to sell him a burial plot and offered an alternative: he could bury his wife in one of their own caves.

17. How did the Hittites refer to Abraham?

_____

_____

Genesis 23:7–13

Abraham pressed on, hoping to buy a particular cave close to the plain of Mamre (Hebron), where he had once resided and built an altar (Gen. 13:18).

Genesis 23:14–20

Finally, title to the field and its cave was transferred to Abraham through a publicly witnessed legal transaction. After living as a transient in the region for some fifty-eight years, Abraham at last became a landowner.

Looking Ahead

With the birth of Isaac, God's plan to create a people for His own special purposes took a giant step forward. Abraham at last had the promised heir who could one day inherit his property and take his place as God's covenant partner.

El Shaddai had not yet made clear, however, just *how* the covenant promises were to be passed on to Isaac. Would he simply inherit them de facto when Abraham died, or would the transfer take place through some event or transaction? Would Isaac have a choice whether to take his father's place as vassal-prince of the Most High?

Table 1. Suzerainty Treaty Pattern

Written suzerainty treaties from the second millennium B.C. typically included the first six elements below. To solemnize, or "cut" a treaty, the vassal swore an oath of loyalty and obedience to his suzerain with a curse for disobedience. [25]

Preamble	Identification and titles of the suzerain
Historical Prologue	Past benefits provided by the suzerain for the vassal-king
Words	Stipulations of the treaty
Storage of Terms	Provision for preservation and periodic reading of the treaty
Witnesses	The god(s) called on to witness the treaty
Blessings and Curses	Rewards (protection, prosperity, health) for obedience; consequences (poverty, disease, disaster, death) for disobedience
Oath-and-Curse	Pledge to obey the stipulations of the treaty, accompanied by a symbolic action depicting the consequences of breaking the oath
Shared Meal	Celebration and finalizing of the new "family" entity
Memorial	A permanent reminder of the treaty

Notes:

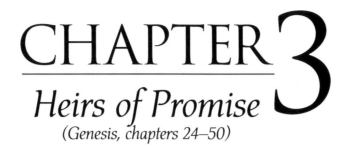

CHAPTER 3
Heirs of Promise
(Genesis, chapters 24–50)

> *But My covenant I will establish with Isaac.*
>
> *—Genesis 17:21 (NIV)*

God's special purposes for Abraham and his descendants required that they remain loyal to Him, rejecting all other gods and religious systems. Only by faithfully preserving and walking in the truth would they inherit the promised blessings.

God had entered into covenant with Abraham in two distinct steps: commitment and ratification. In establishing Isaac and, later, Jacob as heirs to the covenant promises, He would follow the same two-step process. Isaac and Jacob would each have an opportunity to accept or reject God's offer of a covenant relationship.

A Bride for Isaac

Genesis 24:1–67
As a father, Abraham did everything in his power to ensure that Isaac would remain loyal to God. When, according to custom, he sought a bride for Isaac, he turned not to his Canaanite neighbors but to his relatives in far-off Haran.

Abraham prepared a servant to make the journey to Haran, putting him under oath not to return with a Canaanite woman and warning him twice not to let Isaac accompany him on the mission.

Abraham was taking no chance that Isaac might marry and settle down in Haran, away from the land God had promised to him and his descendants. Instead, he trusted God to guide the servant to a young woman who would choose to leave her family and travel over five hundred miles to marry Isaac.

God rewarded Abraham's faith. One evening, as Isaac walked in an open field, he spotted the returning caravan and started toward it. His eyes were fixed on a young woman who had dismounted from her camel and was covering herself with a veil. To forty-year-old Isaac, Rebekah seemed truly a gift from heaven.

Genesis 25:1–11
After Sarah's death, Abraham remarried and had additional sons, but he took special care to ensure that Isaac alone would live in the Land of Promise.

Genesis 25:19–26
Isaac took Rebekah as his wife, but for the next twenty years they remained childless. When Rebekah at last conceived, her pregnancy was difficult.

1. *What did she learn was the cause of her suffering?*

    _____

    _____

2. *Which twin did God say would be stronger and have authority over his brother?*

    _____

    _____

Genesis 25:27–34
The rivalry between Jacob and Esau continued into their young adulthood. Jacob watched for an opportunity to gain his brother's birthright, and, when it came, he acted quickly. His bargain with Esau constituted a legal agreement.

> The birthright of a firstborn son entitled him to preeminence among his siblings and a measure of authority over them, as well as a double portion of his father's estate.[1]

Covenant Offer

Genesis 26:1–6
Isaac sought temporary relief from a drought by migrating to Gerar. There, God appeared to him and offered him the same promises He had once made to Abraham.

3. *What one condition did God attach to His offer?*

_____

_____

4. *What reason did God give for His willingness to pass on the covenant promises to Isaac?*

_____

_____

Because of Abraham's loyalty and faithfulness, the covenant had remained intact and could be passed on to Isaac.

Commitment and Courtship

By choosing to obey God and remain in Gerar, Isaac agreed to serve God as vassal-prince. In the years following Isaac's commitment, God protected him from harm and provided for his well-being even when his faith was weak.

Genesis 26:7–16
In Gerar, when Isaac feared for his life and asked Rebekah to lie about her identity, God protected her and treated him kindly, causing his wealth to increase exponentially. Eventually, Isaac became so prosperous that the Philistines grew jealous.

When, years earlier, Abraham and King Abimelech had concluded a friendship pact, they had expected the treaty to be binding upon their heirs. By expelling Isaac from his territory, the king of Gerar broke that agreement (Gen. 21:22–32).[2]

Genesis 26:17–22
Isaac wandered through the valley in constant search of fresh pasture and water. As a foreigner, he could not claim legal rights to the wells he dug, and when the shepherds of Gerar contested his ownership, he was forced to abandon them and move on.

Blessings Confirmed

Genesis 26:23–25
When at last Isaac returned to the location where his father and Abimelech had made their pact, God appeared to him a second time.

Identifying Himself as "the God of Abraham," He finalized His covenant with Isaac, repeating His promises of protection, favor, and many descendants. With this transaction, God's covenant title expanded to "the God of Abraham and the God of Isaac."

> 5. *How did Isaac affirm his loyalty to God and commemorate the transaction (v. 25)?*

_____

_____

Genesis 26:26–33
Soon after these events, unexpected visitors arrived from Gerar. The king who had so recently expelled Isaac from his territory now requested a nonaggression pact.

> 6. *How did Abimelech explain his change of attitude?*

_____

_____

Recognizing that Isaac had succeeded his father as the one "blessed of the LORD"—i.e., under His protection—King Abimelech sought to mend the relationship he had broken.[3]

The new nonaggression pact was a parity treaty—a covenant between equals. Abimelech and Isaac solemnized the treaty by sharing a feast and swearing oaths.

Succession

Genesis 26:34–35
Neither Esau nor Jacob seemed to share their father's devotion to the Almighty. At age 40, Esau's choice of two Hittite women for wives brought additional discord to the family.

Genesis 27:1–29
When Isaac decided it was time to pronounce the covenant blessings, he sent for Esau, his firstborn son. Rebekah, however, was determined that her favorite, Jacob, would succeed his father as covenant partner of the Most High.

Although Jacob worried that his mother's plan might fail, he went along with it, impersonating Esau in order to obtain the covenant blessings.

God's promises to Abraham had included many descendants, prosperity, protection, land, and the Promised One as a descendant (Gen. 12:1–7). At this time, Isaac pronounced only the blessings of prosperity and protection.

> 7. *How did Isaac word the blessing of protection (v. 29)?*
>
> _____
>
> _____

Genesis 27:30–41
Once given, the covenant blessings could not be retracted. Esau found no comfort in Isaac's "leftover" blessing or in his prophecy that he would one day break free of his brother's authority. Enraged, he vowed to kill Jacob.

Genesis 27:42–28:2
Rebekah concealed the fact that Jacob's life was in danger and persuaded Isaac to send him to Haran to seek a wife among her relatives.

Genesis 28:3–5

> 8. *Before sending Jacob on his way, Isaac pronounced two of the*
> *remaining covenant blessings upon him:*
> *a)* _____ *and*
> *b)* _____ .

> 9. *What was the only blessing Isaac did not pronounce at this time*
> *(Gen. 26:4)?*
>
> _____
>
> _____

In blessing Jacob, Isaac invoked God's name *El Shaddai* (God Almighty), the same name God had used in finalizing His covenant with Abraham (Gen. 17:1).

Jacob now possessed both the birthright of the firstborn son and the covenant blessings, but—would the Almighty confirm Isaac's pronouncements? Would He accept a conniving deceiver as covenant partner? And, would Jacob agree to become the loyal and obedient servant God sought?

Conditional Agreement

Genesis 28:10–15

Separated from all that was familiar, Jacob faced the uncertainty of a long journey into unknown territory. As he slept alone under the stars, God appeared to him in a dream.

Identifying Himself by His name *Yahweh* and by His covenant title, "the God of Abraham your father and the God of Isaac," God offered Jacob the very same promises He had made to Abraham and Isaac—including the promise that the Rescuer would come from among their descendants.

Genesis 28:16–22

> *10. Throughout his life, Jacob had done things his way. When he awoke*
>
> *from his dream, how had his attitude changed?*

_____

_____

Jacob agreed to God's covenant proposal conditionally: if God would provide for him, keep him safe, and bring him back to Canaan, then he would be His servant. During this time, God would watch for evidence of Jacob's loyalty: once he joined his relatives in Haran, would Jacob remain faithful to God, or would he embrace the gods of his kinsmen?

Genesis 29:1–31:2

Jacob spent the next twenty years among his mother's people in Haran, where he married his cousins Leah and Rachel and became the father of eleven sons and a daughter.

In marriage arrangements of the time, it was customary for a groom or his family to pay a bride-price to compensate the bride's family for the loss of her future labor.[4] Jacob labored for fourteen years to pay the bride-prices for Leah and Rachel. During this time, his father-in-law proved to be as selfish, conniving, and deceitful as Jacob himself had once been.

Jacob's Flight from Beersheba to Haran

Homeward Bound

Genesis 31:3

Two decades had passed since Jacob had fled his home in Beersheba. His mother had promised to send for him once Esau's anger abated, but no such summons had come. Then one day, Jacob heard God's voice announce that it was time to return to the land of his birth.

11. *What did God once again promise him?*

_____

_____

12. *In covenant terms, what did this promise signify?*

_____

_____

Genesis 31:4–16

Without delay, Jacob convened a family meeting in the field and announced to Leah and Rachel his intention to return to Canaan. He recounted how Laban had dealt deceitfully with him over the last twenty years and how God had graciously intervened to protect his interests, enabling him to prosper.

Jacob acknowledged that God had met his first two conditions for their covenant partnership (Gen. 28:20–21) and was now close to fulfilling the third: returning him safely to the land of his birth. With both wives in agreement, Jacob assembled their children, gathered the flocks and herds, and departed without notifying his uncle.

Family Matters

Genesis 31:17–42

When Laban caught up with his son-in-law, he expressed outrage at being tricked and deprived of a chance to say good-by to his daughters; but he was also concerned about his missing household gods.

At the time, possession of household gods was a factor in determining inheritance rights. Laban may have worried that, if Jacob had taken the images, he might use them at some future time to make a legal claim on his estate.[5]

Table 2. God's Promises to the Patriarchs

Promises	Abraham *Gen. 12:1–7; 13:16–17*	Isaac *Gen. 26:3–4*	Jacob *Gen. 28:13–15*
Descendants	*And I will make you a great nation... I will make your offspring as the dust of the earth.*	*And I will make your descendants multiply as the stars of heaven.*	*Also your descendants shall be as the dust of the earth.*
Prosperity	*I will bless you and make your name great, and you shall be a blessing.*	*I will be with you and bless you.*	*Behold, I am with you and will keep you wherever you go.*
Protection	*And I will bless those who bless you, and I will curse him who curses you.*	*I will be with you and bless you.*	*Behold, I am with you and will keep you wherever you go.*
The Promised One	*And in you shall all the families of the earth be blessed.*	*And in your seed all the nations of the earth shall be blessed.*	*And in you and in your seed all the families of the earth shall be blessed.*
Land	*To your descendants I will give this land.*	*I will give to your descendants all these lands.*	*The land on which you lie, I will give to you and your descendants.*

Scriptures are from the NKJV.

When Laban failed to find the images, Jacob vented the anger that had built up over the past twenty years.

Genesis 31:43–55
Laban listened and then proposed a treaty.

> *13. Initially, what did Laban say was the purpose for the pact (v. 50)?*

_____

_____

Laban added a nonaggression clause to the treaty, stipulating that in the future neither partner would come against the other to do harm.

To seal the covenant, Jacob erected a pillar and a heap of stones as memorials of the transaction and then shared a meal with his uncle and kinsmen. After swearing an oath, he offered a sacrifice and called for a second feast—an additional affirmation of the pact. Each action was part of the covenant process.

In swearing his oath, Laban called upon more than one god to witness and enforce it; Jacob called only upon *Yahweh*—the God who was the "Fear of his father Isaac."

> Throughout the ancient Near East, sharing a feast was an important step in sealing a treaty. [6]

Danger Ahead

Genesis 32:1–5
Encouraged by a vision of angels, Jacob sent messengers ahead to Esau to announce his return.

As the caravan neared Canaan, however, he became increasingly uneasy. Troubling questions occupied his thoughts: What kind of reception could he expect from Esau? Had his brother's rage abated, or did he still intend to murder him? What could he do to protect his family?

Genesis 32:6–12
The report of Esau approaching with an army of four hundred men confirmed Jacob's fears. He could not flee, and death seemed a very real possibility unless God would truly continue to be with him.

> In blessing Jacob, Isaac had given him authority to rule over his brothers (Gen. 27:29, 37)—the traditional privilege of a firstborn son. Esau's approach at the head of an army signaled that he did not intend to submit to Jacob's authority.

14. After separating the people, the flocks, and the herds into two camps, what did Jacob do?

Jacob appealed to God using the language of a loyal servant-prince petitioning his suzerain for help. Addressing God by His covenant title, "God of my father Abraham and God of my father Isaac" (Gen. 28:13), Jacob first reminded Him that, in returning to Canaan, he was obeying Him.

Then, fully aware that God's mercy was all that stood between him and his brother's sword, Jacob humbly confessed his own unworthiness and acknowledged God's faithfulness to him (Gen. 28:15).

> *15. Of what specific promises did Jacob remind God (v. 12)?*
>
> *a)* _____
>
> *b)* _____

Genesis 32:13-23

After praying, Jacob sent ahead an impressive gift for Esau, selecting over five hundred animals from his flocks and herds. He carefully instructed each shepherd to use the term "lord" when addressing Esau and "servant" when referring to himself, thus implying that he respected his brother's authority as the firstborn.

Contender with God

Genesis 32:24–32

Having sent his family across the river under the cover of night, Jacob remained alone—but not for long.

According to Hosea 12:4, the struggle between the man, or Angel, and Jacob was not entirely physical in nature. As Jacob persisted through the night, he "wept and sought His favor," apparently asking for a blessing that the Angel was not inclined to grant, at least not initially.[7]

What Jacob longed for at this moment was certainty—a guarantee of God's protection, ensuring that he and his family would survive the coming encounter with Esau.

In ancient times, "touching the thigh" was one way to solemnize an oath (Gen. 24:2–3; 47:29–31.) The Angel guaranteed Jacob's safety by touching the hollow of his thigh, but the touch came with such force that Jacob's thigh bone separated from the hip socket.

Jacob, now in pain, persisted in asking for a special blessing and received it. Responding to the Angel's question, he pronounced his name, which meant "heel-catcher" or "supplanter" (Gen. 25:26; 27:36).[9] By giving Jacob a new name, the Angel indicated his elevation to full standing as God's covenant partner. *Israel* means "he strives with God." [10]

> In ancient times, "thigh" was a euphemism for the generative parts. Traditionally, rabbis have interpreted "touching the thigh" in connection with an oath as a reference to circumcision—the sign of God's covenant with Abraham. [8]

Twenty years prior, Jacob had made a conditional pact with God, not yielding Him full control of his life (Gen. 28:20–22). Now, as he looked unconditionally to God to preserve him, he became the fully submitted servant-prince God desired.

The Angel blessed Jacob but did not grant his request that He reveal His name. That event would take place at another time and place, as would the final covenant blessings.

Zero Hour

Genesis 33:1–7
As the brothers came in sight of each other, Jacob's submissive posturing—seven deep bows—had the desired effect.[11] Esau's armed servants likely watched in amazement as their commander embraced his twin.

Genesis 33:8–17
By accepting Jacob's peace offering, Esau committed himself to an amicable relationship. He then allowed Jacob to proceed on his way unaccompanied, expecting that he would follow him back to Seir, southeast of the Dead Sea. Jacob, however, traveled west, toward Succoth; he intended to live apart from Esau.

Genesis 33:18–20
After settling for a time in Succoth, Jacob went on to Shechem and purchased land. There, the name of the altar he built testified to his covenant relationship with the Almighty: *El-elohe-Israel* means "God, the God of Israel." [12]

Genesis 34:1–31

Jacob expected to remain in the vicinity of Shechem, where God had once appeared to his grandfather Abram and promised to give his descendants the land (Gen. 12:6–7). However, when his daughter was raped by the local ruler's son, her brothers secretly plotted revenge. The carnage that followed ended Jacob's plans for a peaceful and prosperous life in that location.

Consecration

Genesis 35:1–4

Fearing retaliation from the neighboring peoples, Jacob was relieved to hear God's voice telling him to journey on to Bethel. Before departing, however, he took care of some unfinished business.

16. *Some of the hired servants had brought small idol-images with them from Mesopotamia. As Jacob prepared to leave for Bethel, what did he order his entire household to do?*

_____

_____

For the first time, Jacob required all those under his authority to consecrate themselves unto God, separating from all other loyalties. He was now determined to govern not only himself but his entire household in ways that pleased his divine Suzerain.

Request Granted

Genesis 35:5–10

17. *How did God protect Jacob and all those with him as they traveled?*

_____

_____

Jacob, now "Israel," built an altar at Bethel, where God had first spoken to him and where he had made his conditional vow (Gen. 28:19–22). By naming the location *El-Bethel* (God of the House of God), he honored the God he now trusted fully for his and his family's safety.

Genesis 35:11–15

In this location, God appeared and at last granted Jacob's request that He reveal His name. *El Shaddai* was the name God had used in ratifying His covenant with Abraham (Gen. 17:1) and the name which Isaac had invoked in blessing Jacob.

El Shaddai finalized His covenant with Jacob, pronouncing the blessings of many descendants and a land of their own. The stone pillar Jacob erected would serve as a lasting memorial of the event.

> God's name *El Shaddai* (God Almighty) appears only six times in the book of Genesis. Each time, it appears in connection with God's covenant with the patriarchs Abraham, Isaac, and Jacob. [13]

Genesis 35:16–29

South of Bethel, Jacob erected another pillar for a much sadder reason. Continuing on without Rachel, but comforted by the birth of Benjamin, he settled in Hebron and was reunited with Isaac before his death at age 180.

Genesis 36:1–8

In time, Esau and Jacob became so wealthy in livestock that the land could not support them both. When Esau voluntarily departed for Edom, Jacob and his sons were left to dwell alone—separated unto God—in the Promised Land (Gen. 25:23).

Dreams and Visions

Genesis 37:1–36; 39:1–45:28

These chapters chronicle the story of Jacob's son Joseph: his dreams, his trials in Egypt, his subsequent rise to power, and his reunion with his brothers during a famine. With Pharaoh's permission, Joseph brought Jacob, his sons, and their families to Egypt so he could provide for them during the remaining years of famine.

Genesis 46:1–4

For the second time in his life, Jacob was leaving the Promised Land, not knowing when or if he would ever return.

At Beersheba, where God had ratified His covenant with Isaac (Gen. 26:24–25), *El Shaddai* appeared to Jacob in "visions of the night" and assured His loyal servant that He would go with him to Egypt. God also confirmed what He had once revealed to Abram—that his descendants would live for a time in Egypt but would eventually return to Canaan (Gen. 15:13–14).

Genesis 47:1–12; 27–31
Israel (Jacob), his sons, and their families settled in Egypt's fertile Delta region.

God had once revealed to Jacob that he would die in Egypt (Gen. 46:4) but Egypt would not be his final resting place. When Jacob sensed that his time was short, he summoned Joseph and asked him to swear an oath to bury him on the family property in Canaan. Carrying out the request would remind all twelve sons that they were not to think of Egypt as their permanent home.

A Double Portion

Genesis 48:1–7
Jacob opened his next meeting with Joseph by reminding him of the covenant blessings *El Shaddai* had pronounced on him at Bethel (Gen. 35:11–12).

> 18. *God had promised to:*
>
> a) _____
>
> _____ *and*
>
> b) _____
>
> _____ .

By adopting Joseph's two sons, Ephraim and Manasseh, Jacob ensured that they would inherit portions of the Promised Land along with their eleven uncles. This transaction alone would provide Joseph with a double portion of Jacob's estate—the privilege of a firstborn son.

Genesis 48:8–22
Jacob then pronounced covenant blessings on Joseph's sons, asking the Shepherd who had protected and blessed him throughout his life to protect, bless, and multiply them as well (vv. 15–16).

> By adopting and blessing Ephraim and Manasseh, Jacob indicated his intention to transfer the rights of the firstborn son from Reuben to Joseph. [14]

Before closing, Jacob assured Joseph that God would be with him and would fulfill His promise to bring him back to the Promised Land (Gen. 15:13–16). He further honored Joseph by giving him the portion of land he still owned in Shechem.

**Table 3. God's Name *El Shaddai* in Genesis:
the Covenant Connection**

Covenant Ratified	Blessings Pronounced	Benefit Claimed	Covenant Remembered
With Abraham *(Gen. 17:1–2)*	On Jacob *(Gen. 28:3–4)*	By Jacob *(Gen. 43:14)*	By Jacob *(Gen. 48:3–4)*
With Jacob *(Gen. 35:11–12)*	On Joseph *(Gen. 49:25–26)*		

Who's Next?

Genesis 49:1–21

Surrounded by all twelve sons, Jacob addressed them in the order of their birth, speaking first to Leah's six sons, then to the sons of her maid, Zilpah, and the sons of Rachel's maid, Bilhah. Last of all, he spoke to Rachel's sons. Only one son would receive the covenant promises, but all twelve hoped to hear blessings of favor and prosperity.

No covenant blessings went to Leah's firstborn son or to the next two in line. Reuben had disqualified himself from the "preeminence of the firstborn" by lying with his father's concubine (Gen. 35:22). Simeon and Levi had earned their father's displeasure by slaying the men of Shechem (Gen. 34:25–29).

To Judah, however, Jacob prophesied that his descendants would include kings who would rule over their brothers and subdue their enemies.

> Genesis 49:10 is understood by many as speaking of the Messiah, the descendant of Judah who, according to prophecy, will one day reign as King over all the earth.

Genesis 49:22–33

Jacob prophesied mostly pleasant futures for each of his next six sons. Then, turning to Joseph, he invoked God by His name *El Shaddai* and pronounced the covenant blessings upon him.

19. How did Jacob describe Joseph in relation to his brothers (v. 26)?

_____

_____

Last of all, Jacob spoke to Rachel's son Benjamin. Then, having commanded his sons to bury him in Canaan, he died.

Genesis 50:1–14

Joseph carried out his oath to bury Jacob in the cave where Abraham, Sarah, Isaac, Rebekah, and Leah now rested (Gen. 47:29–31). He and his brothers, accompanied by a vast entourage of Egyptian royalty, elders, and servants, created an unusual spectacle as they arrived in Canaan.

Genesis 50:15–26

Back in Egypt, the brothers, fearing reprisal from Joseph, lied to him even as they sought his forgiveness. Joseph's gracious response revealed the genuine love he felt for them and his humility before God.

Many years later, when Joseph sensed he was about to die, he reminded his brothers of God's vow to give them the Promised Land and insisted that they take his bones with them when they left Egypt.

20. How did Joseph ensure they would carry out his request (v. 25)?

Slide into Slavery

For a time, the descendants of Jacob (Israel) continued to prosper in Egypt, raising cattle and sheep. They worshipped *El Shaddai,* the God of their fathers, and passed on His promises to their children and grandchildren. Because of their loyalty to Him, they remained a separate people, outside the mainstream of Egyptian society.

Eventually, however, the favor the Israelites had enjoyed during Joseph's lifetime diminished and then disappeared altogether, and they became slaves, just as God had foretold (Gen. 15:12–13).

But He had also foretold their deliverance, and they continued to wait and hope, not knowing how or when God would act—only that He had promised to set them free.

> *But the steadfast love of the LORD is from everlasting to everlasting on those who fear him, and his righteousness to children's children, to those who keep his covenant and remember to do his commandments.*
>
> *—Psalm 103:17–18 (ESV)*

Notes:

CHAPTER 4

Kinsman-Redeemer

(*Exodus, chapters 1–15*)

Dark Times

Exodus 1:1–12

During their years in Egypt, Jacob's descendants multiplied until they numbered between one and two million people. Then, a new pharaoh arose who saw their growing numbers as a threat to the security and stability of his realm.

1. *What did this pharaoh fear would happen if the Hebrews continued to multiply?*

Exodus 1:13–22

When forced labor and increasingly ruthless measures failed to slow the Israelites' growth, the king ordered the Hebrew midwives to kill the newborn male babies.[1]

2. *When the midwives evaded his decree, whom did Pharaoh order to kill the infants?*

Exodus 2:1–10

One young mother secretly kept her infant son alive and was rewarded for her courage when an Egyptian princess adopted him and raised him as her own. Growing up, Moses led a privileged life at court, where he gained the knowledge and experience required for a career within the royal administration.

According to the Jewish historian Flavius Josephus, writing in the first century A.D., Moses served as a general in the Egyptian army and once led a successful campaign against the Ethiopians.[2]

Exodus 2:11–25

As an adult, Moses killed an Egyptian who had been beating a Hebrew slave. He expected his kinsmen to understand he intended to help them; instead, they rejected him. Fearing for his life, he fled the country, leaving behind the privileges, prestige, and authority he had enjoyed as a royal official. As a refugee in Midian, he married, became a father, and settled into a reasonably comfortable and uneventful life, shepherding his father-in-law's flocks.[3]

Meanwhile, the Israelites' situation in Egypt continued to deteriorate, and they cried out to God.

    3.   *What did their cries cause God to remember?*

_____

_____

God had by no means forgotten His covenant with Abraham, Isaac, and Jacob. In this passage, the verb "to remember" (Hebrew, *zakar*) calls attention to the action God is about to take in connection with that covenant.[4]

God had once told Abraham He would fulfill His promise of land when conditions in Canaan reached a tipping point, making it ripe for divine judgment (Gen. 15:16). That time was at hand.

What's in a Name?

Exodus 3:1–8

In Egypt, Moses had sympathized with the suffering of his kinsmen but had been unable to alleviate it. Forty years later, while herding sheep on a remote mountainside, he was given an opportunity to accomplish much more than simply improve their circumstances. God had chosen him to lead the Israelites out of bondage and bring them into the Promised Land.

With his command of the Egyptian language and intimate acquaintance with its culture and political protocol, Moses was eminently qualified for the mission; however, he wanted no part of it.

4. *When God called to Moses from the burning bush, how did He identify Himself?*

_____

_____

Exodus 3:9–12

God had quickly gained Moses' undivided attention, but getting his unqualified consent was another matter. An incredulous Moses balked at the idea of approaching the mighty ruler of Egypt with a petition that he release the Hebrew slaves.

Objections popped into his head, one after another, and God countered them one by one. He began by offering a reassuring promise and a prophecy.

5. *He promised:*

a) _____ *and prophesied that*

b) _____

_____.

Exodus 3:13–15

Moses likely imagined himself facing the elders in Egypt as they peppered him with questions: "Do you know what happens to people who challenge Pharaoh?" "How do we know you've not come to spy on us?" "So, you say the God of our fathers sent you to us—what is His name?"

6. *What was Moses to say when the elders asked him for God's name?*

_____

_____

_____

_____

> God's name *YHWH* means "I AM." Often translated as *Yahweh*, it emphasizes the self-existing nature of God: He is active, eternal Being, without beginning or end. [5]

God had entered into covenant with Abraham, Isaac, and Jacob using His name *El Shaddai* (Almighty God), but it was by His name *Yahweh* that He would judge the Egyptians and bring His people out from under their yoke.[6]

Exodus 3:16–22

In speaking to the elders, Moses was to 1) state God's name and title, 2) tell them God had appeared to him, and 3) announce that God was about to fulfill His promise to deliver them from slavery and bring them into the Promised Land (Gen. 15:13–16).

God graciously previewed for Moses all that was about to transpire in Egypt—the elders' initial reaction, Pharaoh's resistance, and the slaves' eventual plundering of the Egyptians' wealth.

> *And he said to Abram, Know well that your offspring shall be strangers in a land*
> *not theirs, and they shall be enslaved and oppressed four hundred years;*
> *but I will execute judgment on the nation they shall serve,*
> *and in the end they shall go free with great wealth.*
>
> *—Genesis 15:13–14 (JPS)*

When Will You Trust Me?

Exodus 4:1–20

"They won't believe me!" This objection also failed to move God; the signs He gave Moses to perform would reassure skeptics among the elders and confirm that the God of their fathers was indeed "with him."

Still resisting God's call on his life, Moses cited his slowness of speech. Then, abandoning all pretense, he asked God outright to send someone else.

> 7. *How did God counter his excuse of poor speaking ability (v. 12)?*
>
> _____
>
> _____

God brought the meeting on the mountain to an abrupt close, and Moses went home to pack. His very last hope of avoiding the assignment vanished when his father-in-law approved the mission.

Exodus 4:21–23

In His final charge to Moses, God spoke of the Israelites collectively as His "son"—i.e., the people whom He had chosen for a covenant relationship.

Exodus 4:24–28

Moses' failure to have circumcised his own son nearly cost him his life. As a descendant of Abraham, if he did not keep his covenant obligation to God, he would not be allowed to serve as His chosen representative (Gen. 17:9–14).

Pharaoh feared an invasion of foreigners, and that fear was about to be realized, although not in the way he imagined (Ex. 1:10). God had arranged for Moses' older brother, Aaron, to join him at the start of the journey. The "troops" headed for Egypt consisted of two men in their eighties, armed with a rod and God's promise to be with them.

Exodus 4:29–31

> 8. *In Egypt, how did the elders and the people respond when they learned that God had seen their affliction and was taking action?*

_____

_____

Opening Round

Exodus 5:1–5

The Hebrew elders who accompanied Moses and Aaron when they presented their demand to Pharaoh witnessed the king's angry reaction firsthand (Ex. 3:18).

> 9. *What reason did Pharaoh give for refusing to release the slaves?*

_____

_____

In the eyes of Egyptians, Pharaoh was a semi-divine priest-king: he was an incarnation of Horus, son of Osiris, and the son and heir of Re, the sun-god. [7] On his forehead, the pharaoh wore a metal symbol of the sun-god's protection: the flared head of a cobra.

Statue of Rameses II.
©Face_Face/Shutterstock.com

Egyptians recognized more than 2,000 gods, but the God of the Hebrews was not one of them. [8]

Pharaoh took Moses' demand that he bow to the will of *Yahweh*—the God worshiped by an enslaved people—as an insult. He scoffed and then retaliated.

Exodus 5:6–23

Moses, heartsick and dismayed by the punishment Pharaoh inflicted on the Hebrews, thought the mission had failed.

Kinsman-Redeemer

Exodus 6:1–8

In this dark moment, God formally announced His intention to act as Kinsman-Redeemer. He first identified Himself and then proclaimed His promises to liberate the Hebrew slaves, take them as His people, and bring them into the Promised Land.

> *I—Yahweh*
>
> *I will bring you out from under the burdens of the Egyptians, and*
> *I will rescue you from their bondage, and*
> *I will redeem you with an outstretched arm and with great judgments:*
>
> *I will take you as my people, and I will be your God.*
> *Then you shall know that I am the LORD your God,*
> *who brings you out from under the burdens of the Egyptians.*
>
> *And I will bring you into the land,*
> *which I swore to give to Abraham, Isaac, and Jacob; and*
> *I will give it to you as a heritage.*
>
> *I—Yahweh* [9]
>
> *—Exodus 6:6–8 (NKJV)*

God closed His proclamation by repeating His name—in effect, "signing" His declaration.

> *10. How did the Israelites react when Moses presented God's promises to them?*
>
> _____
>
> _____

Exodus 6:9–13

Even though the people did not lay hold of His promises at this time, God would not allow Moses to give up the mission. Once again, He rejected Moses' excuse of poor speaking ability.

Exodus 6:14–30

These verses, listing Moses' and Aaron's lineage, ensured that no other persons could claim to have led the Israelites out of Egypt.

Worldview Clash

When Moses and Aaron approached Pharaoh the second time, the contest began in earnest. Beliefs about the nature of reality lay at the heart of the conflict. The Egyptians and their Hebrew slaves looked at the world through very different lenses.

Egyptians viewed the cosmos as the self-manifestation of a divine energy, or essence, and they believed it was fragile, in perpetual danger of becoming unbalanced and reverting to chaos. [11]

One ancient Egyptian hymn offered praise to the sun-god for making "millions of forms of yourself alone." [10]

Responsibility for maintaining the cosmic order rested primarily with the king. It was his duty to govern in accord with *ma'at*—the system of truth, order, balance, and justice that the first gods had established. [12]

The Egyptian people did their part to uphold *ma'at* by dealing fairly, obeying the king, and causing no disruptions to the social order. Disorder in one area of the cosmos was believed to threaten the stability of the whole. [13]

Nature's cycles—the annual ebb and flow of the Nile, planting season and harvest, and the sun's daily disappearance and "rebirth" were also part of *ma'at*. To ensure their proper functioning, the pharaoh sought the favor of Egypt's chief deities through daily and seasonal rituals.[14] The divine essence—the royal *ka*—was believed to reside in the king, giving him a direct connection to the gods. [15]

Every pharaoh was judged in terms of his success in upholding *ma'at* and maintaining the cosmic order.

The Israelites, on the other hand, saw the universe as the creation of a personal, good, and omnipotent God, who sustained it by His own power. He had created human beings as His image-bearers, and when they rebelled and came under the curse of death, He had promised a Rescuer. This Deliverer was to come from among the descendants of Abraham, Isaac, and Jacob.

Egyptians acknowledged no special calling for the enslaved descendants of Abraham other than to remain at their appointed tasks, obey the king, and cause no disruption to the established order.

In the coming months, as evidence of *Yahweh's* existence and power mounted, Pharaoh would have to choose whether to acknowledge His sovereignty or remain loyal to the Egyptian cosmology. His decision would have disastrous consequences for every Egyptian family.

Table 4. Key Differences in Israelite and Ancient Egyptian Worldviews [16]

Israelite	*Ancient Egyptian*
In the beginning, God.	*In the beginning, a watery, chaotic mass.*
God created the heavens and the earth out of nothing.	*The first god(s) emerged from a watery chaos.*
God is self-existing, personal, and all-powerful, and He sustains the universe by His own power.	*The gods are self-expressions of a divine energy, and none is all-powerful. The cosmos is in constant danger of reverting to chaos.*
God exists independently of the universe.	*The gods exist within the cosmos.*
The natural world is abnormal— altered from its original state.	*The natural world is normal.*
Human nature is fallen.	*Human nature is normal.*
Human beings are created in the image of God and are designed to have a personal relationship with Him.	*Human beings are created to serve the needs of the gods and preserve the cosmic order.*

The Challenge

By demanding a miracle, Pharaoh intended to expose Moses and Aaron as frauds—men who only claimed to be emissaries of a powerful divine Being.

When the magicians' snakes disappeared into the belly of Aaron's serpent, the king's plan backfired. Having lost the high ground, he could no longer underestimate his challengers.

The Plagues

Exodus 7:14–10:29
God's judgments—the ten plagues—brought misery and devastation throughout the land. Coming one after another, each calamity further weakened Pharaoh's position as upholder of the cosmic order.

Moses announced the first, fourth, and seventh plagues by confronting Pharaoh early in the morning, when the sun appeared on the horizon (Ex. 7:15, 8:20, 9:13). The timing dramatized the fact that Moses, as *Yahweh's* emissary, was challenging not only the pharaoh but his supposed protector, the sun-god.

Chronologically, the first nine plagues may have followed Egypt's agricultural season, starting with the annual Nile flood in July and concluding with the final harvest in March. [17]

Exodus 7:14–8:19
By turning the Nile to blood and calling for invasions of frogs and gnats, Moses and Aaron put Pharaoh's magicians in a no-win position. To compete, these officials had to disrupt the natural order the king was sworn to uphold. When they could not replicate the third plague (gnats), they conceded the superior power of Moses' God.

Exodus 8:20–9:12
Only the Egyptians suffered through the next three plagues; the Israelites were spared.

Exodus 9:13–10:23
The seventh and eighth plagues devastated the year's harvests. Some royal officials, losing confidence in Pharaoh's ability to preserve the natural order, heeded Moses' warning to shelter their livestock and servants (Ex. 9:19–20); some urged Pharaoh to concede the battle and release the slaves (Ex. 10:7).

The ninth plague—three days of dense darkness—all but destroyed the king's credibility as defender of *ma'at*.

Exodus 10:24–11:10
The Pharaoh remained adamant in resisting Moses' demands. Negotiations came to an abrupt end when Moses refused to leave behind the Israelites' flocks and herds.

> 11. *At this time, what attitude did Egyptians have toward Moses (Ex. 11:3)?*

In announcing the final plague—the deaths of firstborn sons—Moses predicted that Pharaoh's own servants would bow down before him and order the Israelites to leave Egypt.

Firstborn sons were schooled for leadership; if all died suddenly, there would not be enough trained judges, doctors, scribes, military commanders, and priests to take their places.[18] Pharaoh's intransigence virtually guaranteed the destruction of Egypt's professional class.

A New Beginning

Exodus 12:1–13
The new dating system was to mark permanently the moment in history when God redeemed the Israelites from slavery and betrothed them to Himself. [19]

During the first nine plagues, the Israelites had experienced God's protection without any action required of them.

> 12. *What did God now command families to do in order to protect their firstborn sons?*

Exodus 12:14–20
Before the Passover took place, God gave instructions for commemorating it.

13. *Where did God expect the Israelites to be when they next observed the Passover rites?*

_____

_____

Exodus 12:21-28

Months earlier, the Israelites had ignored God's promise of deliverance (Ex. 6:9). Now, they embraced it. The people listened to Moses' instructions, bowed their heads, worshipped, and then acted. By applying the blood of a lamb to the doorposts and lintels of their homes, the Israelite families took the first step in becoming the "people of *Yahweh*"—a nation set apart to His special purposes.

Suddenly

Exodus 12:29–42

That night, as Egyptian families cried out in mourning for the loss of their firstborn sons, Pharaoh yielded to Moses' demands.

14. *When Pharaoh ordered the Hebrews out of Egypt, what favor did he ask of Moses?*

_____

_____

The mighty Pharaoh at last "knew" the God of the Hebrews—i.e., acknowledged His existence, sovereignty, and superior power.

15. *Why did the Egyptians urge the Israelites to leave immediately (v. 33)?*

_____

_____

The Israelites did leave suddenly, accompanied by a multitude of non-Israelites. They departed with "spoils"—silver, gold, and clothing in abundance—just as God had prophesied to Abraham centuries ago (Gen. 15:13–14).

Exodus 12:43–51

The large number of non-Israelites who left Egypt along with the Hebrews created a potential problem. Should people who were not lineal descendants of Abraham be allowed to participate in the annual memorial celebrations?

> 16. *What was to be required of non-Israelite families before*
>   *they could participate?*

_____

_____

Circumcision implied a vow of loyalty and obedience to *Yahweh* (Gen. 17:9–10). Only by first making this commitment could outsiders be accepted as members of the covenant family.

Remember!

Exodus 13:1–16
Human memories can be short, and God charged the Israelites to remember His mighty work of delivering them from slavery in Egypt. In the future, they were to observe the Passover and the Feast of Unleavened Bread annually and explain these memorials to their children, instilling in them a sense of gratitude and loyalty to their divine Kinsman-Redeemer. In addition, when a family celebrated the arrival of a firstborn son, they were to observe a special memorial.

> 17. *How were the parents of a firstborn son to commemorate God's*
>   *deliverance of the firstborn sons of His people in Egypt?*

_____

> *It is a night to be much observed unto the LORD for bringing them*
> *out of Egypt; this is that night of the LORD to be observed of all the*
> *children of Israel in their generations.*
>
> —*Exodus 12:42 (KJV)*

En Route

Exodus 13:17–22
On very short notice, between one and two million Israelites departed Egypt in an orderly fashion.[20] Such a feat could only have been accomplished through careful and extensive planning.[21] They left as a betrothed nation—a chosen people, set apart to God and traveling under His protection, with a pillar of cloud to lead them by day and a pillar of fire by night.

18. *What centuries-old vow did the Israelites fulfill as they left (Gen. 50:24–25)?*

_____

_____

Exodus 14:1–12

The route Moses and the Israelites took from Egypt to Midian is still debated. They avoided the well-traveled road that hugged the Mediterranean coast (Ex. 13:17), but did they head south and east, around the tip of the Sinai Peninsula, or did they instead cross the midsection of the Sinai, intending to skirt the northern tip of the Gulf of Aqaba?

At one point, the Israelites obeyed God's instructions to turn south and camp facing the Red Sea. However, Pharaoh had sent his army in pursuit, and as the Egyptian troops came into view, the Israelites found themselves trapped, with no way of escape.

> According to the historian Josephus, rugged, impassable mountains hemmed the Israelites in on two sides of their camp, and the Egyptian army blocked retreat to the rear. [22]

19. *How did the people react as the Egyptian army closed in?*

_____

_____

Exodus 14:13–22

As Moses obeyed God and stretched out his rod over the Sea, the waters parted, and the Israelites walked on dry ground throughout the night to the opposite shore.

20. *How did God keep the Egyptians from coming near the Israelites?*

_____

_____

Exodus 14:23–31

Pharaoh, the "son of the sun-god," had hoped to force the Hebrew slaves to return. Ironically, his hope perished as the sun's first rays brightened the eastern horizon and towering walls of water imploded on his troops, sweeping them away in a watery chaos.

As the calm of early morning returned and the waves lapped the sand in their accustomed cadence, the dead bodies of Egyptian soldiers began to wash up on the beach.

Exodus 15:1–21
Safe on land, the Israelites realized they were at last truly free. Led by Moses and Miriam, they sang praises to *Yahweh*, recounted His mighty acts, and rejoiced in their deliverance.

> *Or has God ever tried to go and take for Himself a nation from the midst of another nation, by trials, by signs, by wonders, by war, by a mighty hand, by an outstretched arm, and by great terrors, as the Lord your God did for you in Egypt before your eyes?*
>
> *To you it was shown, that you might realize and have personal knowledge that the Lord is God; there is no other besides Him.*
>
> *—Deuteronomy 4:33–34 (AMP)*

Notes:

> *I am the LORD.*
>
> *I will bring you out from under the burdens of the Egyptians, and*
> *I will rescue you from their bondage, and*
> *I will redeem you with an outstretched arm and with great judgments:*
>
> *I will take you as my people, and I will be your God.*
> *Then you shall know that I am the LORD your God,*
> *who brings you out from under the burdens of the Egyptians.*
>
> *And I will bring you into the land,*
> *which I swore to give to Abraham, Isaac, and Jacob;*
> *and I will give it to you as a heritage.*
>
> *I am the LORD.*
>
> *—Exodus 6:6–8 (NKJV)*

God had promised to free the Israelites from bondage, take them to be His people, and give them the land of Canaan as an inheritance. Phase two of His three-part plan— taking them as His people—had begun with the Passover in Egypt and would culminate at Mount Sinai. As the Israelites journeyed through the wilderness toward Mount Sinai, God would have opportunities to "get to know" His prospective vassal-nation before finalizing His covenant with them.

Kindnesses

In covenant parlance, a suzerain's benevolent acts or gifts were known as "kindnesses," and to accept them was to incur at the very least a debt of gratitude. The Bible records three times when God bestowed kindnesses on His chosen people in the wilderness, supplying their needs in miraculous ways. In each instance, He watched for evidence of their gratitude, loyalty, and trust.

Kindness #1: Fresh Springs of Water

Exodus 15:22–27

After walking through arid country for three days, the Israelites found only a polluted source of water for themselves and their livestock. Instead of remembering God's promises and looking to Him for aid, they blamed Moses for their circumstances.

When Moses prayed, God revealed both how to purify the water and how the people could enjoy continuing good health.

1. *God's blessing of well-being was contingent on their conduct. He would keep them healthy if they:*

    a) _____

    b) _____

    c) _____ *and*

    d) _____.

2. *How did God chasten the people for grumbling and failing to rely on Him?*

    _____

Kindness #2: Daily Manna

Exodus 16:1–21

After a month of camping, people began to recall life in Egypt as having been "not so bad." At the very least, it had been predictable, with meat, bread, and fresh vegetables available daily.

As food became scarce, the Israelites again failed to seek God for their needs and vented their frustration on Moses and Aaron.

3. *Against whom did Moses say they were actually grumbling (v. 8)?*

    _____

Instead of expressing anger or disappointment, God gave Moses good news, tempered by a warning: the people would soon have plenty to eat; however, He would test their willingness to follow instructions.

Because Moses and Aaron announced God's promise of an abundant food supply, no one was able to attribute the arrival of the quails and manna to chance or to the benevolence of another deity.

Exodus 16:22–30

Some Israelites kept the manna overnight, and it spoiled; yet on the sixth day, when they gathered enough for two days, it stayed fresh. Moses explained to the elders that God was instituting a Sabbath, a holy day of rest.

From then on, the people were to gather a double portion of manna on the sixth day. The seventh day was to be set apart to rest and honor *Yahweh*, the God who had created all things in six days and rested on the seventh.

> 4. *How did God punish those Israelites who went out to gather manna on the Sabbath?*

Exodus 16:31–36

God was able to preserve the manna not for two days only but for centuries. A portion was to be kept as a testimony to His faithfulness in meeting the needs of His chosen people.

> *If you turn back your foot from the Sabbath, from doing your pleasure on my holy day, and call the Sabbath a delight and the holy day of the* L<small>ORD</small> *honorable;*
> *if you honor it, not going your own ways, or seeking your own pleasure, talking idly, then you shall take delight in the* L<small>ORD</small>, *and I will make you ride on the heights of the earth;*
> *I will feed you with the heritage of Jacob your father, for the mouth of the* L<small>ORD</small> *has spoken.*
>
> —*Isaiah 58:13–14 (ESV)*

Kindness #3: Water from the Rock

Exodus 17:1–7
At Rephidim, the Israelites once again vilified Moses, blaming him for their circumstances, and *Yahweh* again supplied their need. The elders who accompanied Moses to the rock were eyewitnesses of the miracle.

In three critical situations, the Israelites had proved to have short memories, a lack of trust, and a shallow sense of gratitude. Yet God continued to demonstrate His lovingkindness and faithfulness to them.

First Fight

Exodus 17:8–16
When the Israelites were attacked by the Amalekites, Moses' uplifted rod—the symbol of God's power and authority—was the key to victory. When it pointed up to heaven, the Israelites prevailed; when Moses lowered his arm, the Amalekites prevailed.

In this first battle, the Israelites learned that their enemies were God's enemies and that they would triumph not in their own strength but only as they fought under the name and authority of *Yahweh*—i.e., under His standard, or banner.

Family Reunion

Exodus 18:1–12
When Jethro, accompanied by Moses' wife and sons, arrived at Mount Sinai, he listened attentively as Moses recounted what God had done in Egypt. Then, he took decisive action.

> 5. *How did Jethro indicate he now worshipped the God of his son-in-law?*
>
> _____
>
> _____

By sharing a meal, Moses, Aaron, and the tribal elders celebrated Jethro's faith in *Yahweh*, the God who had delivered the Israelites from slavery in Egypt. [1]

Exodus 18:13–36

Jethro's plan for organizing the judicial system would make Moses' task much easier. Once implemented, it would provide an estimated 78,600 judges to assist Moses in settling disputes.[2] He would handle only the most difficult cases.

Covenant Proposal

> *When you have brought the people out of Egypt, you shall serve God on this mountain.*
>
> *—Exodus 3:12 (NKJV)*

Exodus 19:1–8

Over the course of several weeks, God had demonstrated His goodness, faithfulness, and mercy to His chosen people, and the time had come for a decision. Would they pledge their loyalty and obedience to Him as Suzerain? Would they "cut a covenant?"

The covenant proposal Moses presented to the elders opened with a prologue stating God's past beneficial acts on behalf of the Israelites—a reminder that they were indebted to Him for their lives and freedom.

> 6. *God's offer was conditional: if the Israelites kept the covenant terms,*
>
>   *then they would be (vv. 5–6):*
>
>   a) _____ ,
>
>   b) _____ , and
>
>   c) _____ .

Over the next several days, Moses, now in his eighties, would ascend and descend the rocky slopes of Mount Sinai multiple times, carrying God's messages to the people and relaying their responses back to Him (Ex. 3:12). This time, he reported that the elders and the people had accepted the covenant proposal.

In the ancient Near East, only kings claimed a special relationship with the chief gods. In Israel, by contrast, every individual was offered a personal relationship with *Yahweh.* [3]

Exodus 19:9–15
Next, God called for preparations to finalize the contract. Clean clothing was in order, along with minds focused on the commitment they were about to make.

Exodus 19:16–25
Flames and smoke enveloped Mt. Sinai as the sovereign King and Creator of the universe descended upon it. At the same time, those gathered at the base of the mountain had their senses bombarded by claps of thunder, bolts of lightning, the smell of smoke, earth tremors coming from the mountain itself, and the continuous, penetrating sound of the *shofar,* or ram's horn.

> *The earth shook, the heavens also dropped rain at the presence of God: Sinai itself was moved at the presence of God, the God of Israel.*
>
> *—Psalm 68:8 (NKJV)*

The Ten Words

Exodus 20:1–17
Speaking directly to the people, God identified Himself as "the Lord your God, who brought you out of the land of Egypt, out of the house of slavery." Every Israelite, as well as the strangers that came with them, heard God's voice.

The stipulations, or terms, of a suzerain-vassal treaty were known as the "Words" of the suzerain. God's ten Words, or Commandments, described the conduct He would expect of His people.[4]

The first three Words dealt with the requirement of exclusive loyalty.

> The verbs in all ten Words are in the simple future indicative tense, not the imperative.

1) You shall have no other gods before Me.

God expected His people to forsake all other gods and remain loyal to Him alone. Loyalty was the most-desired quality in a vassal.

The Canaanites worshipped many gods and saw divinity in virtually every aspect of the natural world. The Israelites were to reject both the Canaanite gods and the premise of a divinity-infused natural order.[5]

2) You shall not make for yourself a carved image, or any likeness of anything that is in heaven above, or that is in the earth beneath, or that is in the water under the earth. You shall not bow down to them or serve them.

The purpose of a carved or molded idol-image was to attract a divine energy—a deity—to inhabit it and exert a beneficial influence in a given locale. Throughout the ancient Near East, priests "cultivated" a god's presence by placing its image in a restful environment and supplying its supposed daily needs for food, a bath, and ritual incantations.[6]

The Israelites were to reject both the concept of god-infused images and the idea that human beings could meet the needs of a deity.[7]

3) You shall not take the name of the LORD your God in vain, for the LORD will not hold him guiltless who takes his name in vain.

Upon entering into covenant with *Yahweh*, the Israelites would "take" His name, becoming "the people of *Yahweh*." They were not to dishonor His name by their conduct or by breaking their vow of loyalty to Him alone.

Kiddush ha-Shem, Hebrew for "sanctification of God's name," means behavior that is worthy of God and reflects who He is. The opposite, *chillul ha-Shem,* refers to behavior that desecrates God's name. [8]

When swearing oaths, the Israelites were to invoke only the name of *Yahweh*, and they were to perform all their vows (Lev. 9:12; Josh. 9:18–19).

The next two Words called for positive actions: "You shall" rather than "You shall not."

4) Remember the Sabbath day, to keep it holy. Six days you shall labor, and do all your work, but the seventh day is a Sabbath to the LORD your God.

Sabbath observance would be a sign of Israel's covenant relationship with the God who had created the heavens and the earth in six days and rested on the seventh (Ex. 31:13). As an institution, it would be unique to "the people of *Yahweh*;" no other nation of the time is known to have observed a weekly day of rest.[9]

5) Honor your father and your mother, that your days may be long in the land that the LORD *your God is giving you.*

This Word is explicitly connected with a blessing for God's people: the enjoyment of many days—long life—in the Promised Land (Deut. 5:16, 33).

Exodus 20:13–17
The remaining five Words prohibited behavior and attitudes which are contrary to the character of God and which, if condoned, would make the goal of a just and happy society unattainable.

> 7. *If God had given these five commandments in positive terms, how might He have worded them?*
>
> *6) You shall not murder.*[10] _____
>
> _____
>
> *7) You shall not commit adultery.* _____
>
> _____
>
> *8) You shall not steal.* _____
>
> _____
>
> *9) You shall not bear false witness against your neighbor.* _____
>
> _____
>
> *10) You shall not covet...anything that is your neighbor's.* _____
>
> _____
>
> _____

Exodus 20:18–21
Fear gripped many Israelites as they experienced the sights and sounds coming from Mount Sinai. Moses assured them that God's intention was to produce not terror but a reverential awe, so they would be mindful in the future to do what was right in His sight (Ex. 20:20).

A Holy Nation

> *You shall be holy to me; for I the LORD am holy and have separated you from the peoples, that you should be mine.*
>
> —*Leviticus 20:26 (ESV)*

Exodus 20:22–23:19

The additional directives God gave to Moses applied the values set forth in the first ten Words to everyday life. Protections for life, property, and reputation were high priorities, as were the needs of the fatherless, widows, and temporary residents. Justice was to be administered impartially, without favoritism.

> 8. *Why did God direct the Israelites to treat temporary residents with kindness (Gen. 22:21)?*

_____

_____

Exodus 23:20–33

Before sending Moses back down the mountain, God previewed what the Israelites could expect once they had sworn to be "the people of *Yahweh*." He began with a warning: until now, their complaining and disobedience had been graciously overlooked; after they cut the covenant, they would be held accountable for such behavior. By heeding the Angel's voice, however, they could expect blessings of protection, provision, health, many children, and long life.

Once in the Promised Land, they were to follow a zero-tolerance policy toward the Canaanites' worship practices and way of life.[11] Refusing all offers of friendship treaties, they were to press on until God had driven all their enemies out of the land.

> *I am the LORD your God.*
>
> *You shall not do as was done in the land of Egypt, where you lived, and you shall not do as they do in the land of Canaan to which I am bringing you. You shall not walk in their statutes. You shall follow my rules and keep My statutes and walk in them.*
>
> *I am the LORD your God.*
>
> —*Leviticus 18:2–4 (ESV)*

The Covenant Oath

Exodus 24:1–8

After the Israelites accepted the covenant terms, Moses made a written record of the agreement and began preparations for its ratification. The altar and the twelve pillars he erected, one for each tribe, would remain as memorials of the event long after it took place.

To cut the covenant, Moses dashed half the blood of the sacrificed animals against the altar and then read the terms of the covenant. The Israelites vowed to obey them, and, as Moses sprinkled the remaining blood on them, the covenant was finalized. The descendants of Abraham, Isaac, and Jacob became "the people of *Yahweh*"—a nation chosen and set apart to God and His purposes.[12]

Exodus 24: 9–11

Next, Moses and Aaron, accompanied by Aaron's two sons and seventy Israelite elders, climbed Mount Sinai and shared a special meal in the very presence of God. Representing all the Israelites, they celebrated the nation's new standing as the "family of God."

Table 5. Covenant Pattern at Mt. Sinai

The covenant enactment at Mt. Sinai followed the general pattern of suzerainty treaties from the Late Bronze Age (1550–1200 B.C.).[13]

Preamble	Identity of suzerain	Ex. 20:2
Historical Prologue	Past beneficial deeds of suzerain	Ex. 20:2
Words	Stipulations of the treaty	Ex. 20:3–23:19
Blessings	Rewards promised for obedience	Ex. 23:20–33
Oath-and-Curse	Vassal's pledge to obey covenant stipulations	Ex. 24:3–8
Shared Meal	Celebration of "family" relationship	Ex. 24:9–11
Memorial	Permanent reminder of treaty	Ex. 24:4, 12
Storage of Covenant	Preservation of written treaty	Ex. 25:10–22

Inscribed in Stone

Exodus 24:12–31:18

After the covenant meal, Moses spent an additional forty days and nights on the mountain, where God gave him a "blueprint" for a tabernacle and instructions for ordaining Aaron and his sons as priests. God's Presence would reside in the sanctuary, and there He would continue to meet with Moses and the people.

Lastly, God charged Moses to teach the importance of Sabbath observance as a covenant sign between God and His people throughout their generations.

God presented to Moses two stone "tablets of the testimony," which He had inscribed on both sides. The ten Words and the additional directives were to serve as Israel's founding document, enabling them to build a society that would reflect God's goodness and wisdom.

The stone tablets would provide a permanent record of the covenant terms, which could be consulted as needed.

In other nations, rulers and common people alike sometimes struggled to know how to please or appease their gods.[14] By contrast, the Israelites would have a written contract that stated clearly what *Yahweh* expected of them. If they learned and faithfully applied His laws and ordinances, they would prosper as a nation.[15]

> *For what great nation is there who has a god so near to them as the Lord our*
> *God is to us in all things for which we call upon Him?*
> *And what large and important nation has statutes and ordinances so upright*
> *and just as all this law which I set before you today?*
>
> *—Deuteronomy 4:7–8 (AMP)*

Notes:

CHAPTER 6
The Promised Land
(Exodus, chapters 32–40, with portions of
Leviticus, Numbers, Deuteronomy, and Joshua)

Crisis

Exodus 32:1–6
Moses expected to return to camp and begin teaching the Law while the sanctuary was under construction. Once it was dedicated, he would lead the Israelites on to Canaan, where they would gradually take possession of the Promised Land.

Unfortunately, those expectations were soon obliterated. During Moses's absence, Aaron had given in to the demands of the people for a molten image to worship.

Exodus 32:7–14
When God informed Moses of the rebellion, He spoke of the Israelites no longer as His people but as Moses' people. They had broken the covenant and merited His wrath.

Thinking quickly, Moses pointed out that, if God were to consume the nation in anger, the Egyptians would "spin" the news in a way that would make Him appear capricious and evil. God's name—His reputation—was at stake.

> 1. *What did Moses then ask God to remember?*
>
> _____
>
> _____

Exodus 32:15–35
Accompanied by Joshua, Moses returned to the camp, carrying the stone tablets God had inscribed. There, incensed by what he saw and heard, he broke the tablets, destroyed the golden calf, and called for execution of the rebels. The next day, he climbed back up the mountain to try to repair the broken relationship between God and the people but did not succeed. God rejected his petition for forgiveness at this time. [1]

Exodus 33:1–6

God directed Moses to lead the Israelites to Canaan but announced He would not go with them.

    2.   *What reason did God give for His decision not to go with them?*

_____

_____

Persistent Hope

Exodus 33:7–11

Moses made no immediate effort to prepare the Israelites for departure. Instead, he continued to seek God in prayer, retreating regularly to a "tent of meeting" at the edge of camp. There God met and spoke with him "as a man speaks to his friend."

The broken relationship between God and His people was of primary concern to Moses, along with the coming journey to Canaan. Did God still consider the Israelites to be His chosen people? Was there yet hope that He might forgive them, renew the covenant, and accompany them to the Promised Land?

    3.   *How did the people now show a) their respect for Moses and b) their reverence for God?*

        a) _____

_____

        b) _____

_____

Exodus 33:12–17

At some point, Moses put his concerns in God's hands and asked only to be shown His way—whatever it might be—and to know Him on a deeper, more intimate level. God responded with a gracious promise: He would go with Moses as he led the Israelites to Canaan.

Encouraged, Moses pressed on, seeking grace and reinstatement for all the people. In presenting his case, Moses intentionally linked himself with the Israelites, twice using the phrase "I and Your people."

Exodus 33:18–23
Finally, Moses made known his heart's desire: to see God's glory.

A Suzerain's Love

Exodus 34:1–9
In Hebrew, the words "merciful" and "gracious" describe someone whose actions arise out of a deep love, loyalty, and compassion, such as a father feels for his children.[2] God's choice of words seemed to signal that He was willing to forgive His people. Seizing the opportunity, Moses boldly asked God to restore them to their former standing.

Exodus 34:10–28
Moses' petition was granted. In renewing the covenant, God summarized its key terms, emphasizing the requirement of exclusive loyalty. The "people of *Yahweh*" were not to enter into pacts with the Canaanite peoples or acknowledge their gods in any way. They were to gather together three times a year to commemorate His goodness, faithfulness, and mighty acts on their behalf. Only if the Israelites remembered *whose* people they were, could they hope to prosper in the Promised Land.

Exodus 34:29–35
Carrying the freshly inscribed stone tablets, Moses returned to camp and with shining countenance spoke first to the elders and then to the entire congregation.

Sanctuary: Design and Purpose

Exodus 35:1–36:7
A wave of relief likely passed through the congregation as Moses charged them to keep the Sabbath and then asked for donations of material and laborers for the sanctuary. His words confirmed that God had forgiven the transgression of His people and intended to dwell among them.

The subsequent outpouring of goods and volunteers for the project was proof of the Israelites' renewed love and commitment to *Yahweh*. Moses soon had to call a halt to donations because the workmen had far more than they needed to complete the work.

Model of the Ark of the Covenant.
© George Dukinas/Shutterstock.com.

Exodus 36:8–39:43

The sanctuary instructions called for a wood frame structure enclosed by curtains on all sides and covered by four layers of cloth and waterproof skins. Inside, a thickly woven curtain would divide the space into two rooms.

In the innermost room, a hardwood chest would provide storage for the stone tablets of the covenant. The chest was to be encased in pure gold and have a lid of solid gold, adorned with two golden figures of cherubim facing each other.

God had promised to dwell between the cherubim and to speak with Moses in that location (Ex. 25:8, 21–22).

The sanctuary, along with its courtyard, was to be the spiritual center of the new nation, where people would gather on feast days and other holy days to commemorate their heritage, bring offerings, and worship *Yahweh*.

Exodus 40:1–33

The Israelites' second year as a free people began with the dedication of the tabernacle and the consecration of Aaron and his sons as priests.

4. *By what means were the tent, its furnishings, and its priests to be consecrated?*

_____

_____

Exodus 40:34–38

When the glory cloud of God's Presence covered and filled the sanctuary, even Moses could not enter. In the days and years ahead, the Presence of God in the cloud and in fire remained with His chosen people, blessing, protecting, and guiding them as they traveled through the wilderness.

Maintain the Relationship

God had promised to dwell with His people, and the Israelites had sworn to walk in His ways. Inevitably, however, people would fall short, failing to keep His laws and ordinances perfectly.

How would the covenant relationship between a holy God and a nation of fallen individuals be maintained? Could God be just and also merciful to sinners? Was there a way for a transgressor to be forgiven and restored to a right relationship with God?

Answers were found in the system of sacrifices and offerings God instituted at Sinai before the Israelites departed for Canaan. His instructions to Moses, recorded in the book of Leviticus, describe how His people were to atone for their sins when they had broken their covenant vows.

Atonement by a Substitute

Leviticus 1:1–17; 4:1–7:38
When a person sinned and subsequently sought forgiveness, he was to bring a healthy young animal from the herd or flock to the altar opposite the door of the tabernacle and kill it there. A priest—Aaron or one of his sons—would then apply the blood to the altar and, in the case of a burnt offering, burn the body on the altar.

> 5. *How was the person to signify he identified with the animal?*

The innocent animal would die as a substitute, bearing the guilt of the person who offered it. Its death would be accepted as atonement for sin, and the sinner would be forgiven (Lev. 17:11). [3]

Yom Kippur (Day of Atonement)

Leviticus 16:1–34
Once each year, on *Yom Kippur,* the high priest was to atone for the sins of the whole congregation. While the people fasted and prayed, repenting for their offenses, the priest was to enter the Most Holy Place and sprinkle the blood of a bull and a goat on the *kapporet*—the solid gold lid that covered the Ark. Then, laying his hands on the head of a live goat, he was to confess the sins of the people and send the goat into the wilderness.

> The words *kapporet* and *kippur* (as in *Yom Kippur*) both derive from a Hebrew word meaning "to atone by offering a substitute." [4]

Additional Sacrifices

Leviticus 17:1–8

All sacrifices and offerings were to be made in only one location—at the door to the tent of meeting.

> 6. *Why did God forbid the offering of sacrifices away from the tabernacle?*
>
> _____
>
> _____

Leviticus 23:4–44

In addition to daily offerings of year-old lambs, sacrifices were to be offered on special holy days, including Passover, the Feast of Firstfruits, and the Feast of Weeks.

The sacrificial system, while keeping the nation mindful of the need to "be holy, as God is holy" (Lev. 19:2), would require the death of many animals over the course of a year. Eventually, some of God's people may have longed for a time when sacrifices would no longer be necessary, but—could it ever be? Only God knew.

> Since the Garden of Eden, those who worshipped *Yahweh* associated the sacrifice of an animal with God's mercy and His promise of a Rescuer. The patriarch Job, for example, offered sacrifices to atone for his children's sins, and he looked forward to the day when his Redeemer would stand upon the earth (Job 1:5, 19:25).

A Charge to Keep

Numbers 2:1–34; 10:11–36

In preparation for the journey from Mount Sinai to the Promised Land, Moses assigned the tribes their order of departure; when the cloud of God's Presence lifted, the people were ready to follow.

Numbers 11:1–14:38

The journey should have taken less than two weeks, but further disobedience and rebellion caused the Israelites to spend thirty-eight additional years wandering from place to place. All those who had come out of Egypt as adults eventually perished in the wilderness, with two exceptions: Caleb and Joshua lived to enter the Promised Land.

Deuteronomy 1:1–30:20

At last, as the new generation of Israelites camped on the east bank of the Jordan, ready to cross over into Canaan, Moses addressed them in a series of heartfelt sermons. He recounted their history and charged them to love God with all their hearts, teach their children His ways, and obey His laws.

By so doing, they would prosper and become a lighthouse of blessing and truth in a dark world.

Moses' addresses, as recorded in the book of Deuteronomy, fit the pattern of a covenant agreement—in this case, a covenant *renewal* for the new generation of Israelites. However, he directed that one component of the renewal was not to be carried out immediately.

The Israelites were not to pronounce the covenant blessings and curses until they possessed Mount Gerizim and Mount Ebal, overlooking the city of Shechem in Canaan.

Table 6. Covenant Renewal

Preamble (Deut. 1:1–5)

Historical Prologue (Deut. 1:6–4:43)

Words (Deut. 4:44–26:15)

Oath (Deut. 26:16–19; 29:10–15)

Permanent Memorial (Deut. 27:1–8)

Blessings and Curses (Deut. 27:9–28:68)

Witnesses (Deut. 30:19–20)

Storage and Periodic Reading (Deut. 31:9–13, 24–26)

Mount Ebal, viewed from Mount Gerizim.
©Hanan Isachar/Isachar-photography.com

Farewell

Deuteronomy 31:1–34:12

Moses' last two assignments were to commission Joshua as his successor and to teach the Israelites a song chronicling God's relationship with them. The song prophesied their future rebellion yet assured them of *Yahweh's* enduring love and compassion (Deut. 32:1–43).

Finally, having spoken prophetic blessings upon each tribe, Moses climbed Mount Nebo and surveyed the Promised Land from a distance. Because he had once dishonored God before all the people (Num. 20:1–13), God did not permit him to cross the Jordan. Moses died on the mountain at age 120 and was buried in the valley.

Aaron, too, had died (Deut. 10:6), and it was Joshua, Moses' faithful assistant, who led the Israelites on into the Promised Land.

Joshua 1:1–8:29

After conquering Jericho and Ai, Joshua followed Moses' instructions and built an altar of uncut stones on Mount Ebal. He offered sacrifices and inscribed the words of the Law on large stones that had been covered with plaster. Then, as half the tribes stood in front of Mount Ebal and half in front of Mount Gerizim, facing the valley and the Levite priests who bore the Ark of the Covenant, Joshua read the Book of the Law for all to hear, and the covenant blessings and curses were pronounced (Deut. 27:1–28:68; Josh. 8:30–35).

The event took place in the same locale where, centuries earlier, God had appeared to a newly arrived immigrant named Abram and promised to give his descendants the land.

Expecting

In the years that followed, as the Israelites took possession of the land, all but one of God's promises to Abraham were fulfilled.

His one remaining promise—to send a Kinsman-Redeemer—continued to be a mystery:

Who would He be?
When and where would He appear?
How would He be recognized?
What would He do to defeat the enemy, Satan?

Notes:

CHAPTER 7

The Promised One
(Prophecies of the Messiah in the Old Testament)

Connect the Clues

In the Garden of Eden, Adam and Eve disobeyed God and brought the curse of death on themselves and their descendants (Gen. 2:16). Succeeding generations inherited their fallen human nature and all the ills that came with it.

God in His mercy promised a Rescuer—a Kinsman-Redeemer—yet provided only two details about His mission: He would one day crush Satan's head under his feet, and He would be wounded in the heel (Gen. 3:15).

Additional details came to light many centuries later, as God revealed them to His chosen people. In the Bible, these clues are scattered like jewels among the historical books, the Psalms, and the writings of the prophets. When connected, they shed light on the mystery of the Messiah—His identity, offices, and mission.

Genealogy

> *In your offspring shall all nations of the earth be blessed.*
>
> —*Genesis 22:18*

Genesis 22:15–18, 26:1–4, 28:10–15
God promised Eve a descendant who would defeat the enemy, Satan. Much later, God promised Abraham, Isaac, and Jacob that one of their descendants would be a blessing to all peoples.[1]

The Scripture selections below contain additional clues about the genealogy of the Messiah. After reading each selection, a) record the name of the individual who is to be an ancestor and b) summarize what is prophesied about the Promised One.

1. *Genesis 49:10*

    a) _____

    b) _____

    _____

2. *Micah 5:2*

    a) _____

    b) _____

    _____

3. *Psalm 89:3-4, 35-36*

    a) _____

    b) _____

    _____

4. *Jeremiah 23:5–6*

    a) _____

    b) _____

    _____

5. *Isaiah 7:13–14*

    a) _____

    b) _____

    _____

6. *Psalm 2:7–8*

    a) _____

    b) _____

    _____

According to these Scriptures, the ancestors of the Promised One will include Abraham, Isaac, Jacob, Judah, and David; He will be born to a woman who is a virgin, and He will be God's Son—*Immanuel,* "God with us."

> *Who has ascended to heaven and descended?*
> *Who has gathered the wind in his fists?*
> *Who has bound the waters in His garment?*
> *Who has established all the ends of the earth?*
> *What is His name, and what is His Son's name, if you know?*
>
> —*Proverbs 30:4 (AMP)*

Offices: Prophet, Priest, and King

In ancient Israel, priests, kings, and sometimes prophets were anointed with oil at their installation ceremonies. The oil symbolized God's authority and the enabling presence of His Holy Spirit. These leaders were then recognized as having been chosen by God, set apart for a specific role, and empowered by His Spirit to carry it out.[2]

In Hebrew, "anointed" is *mashiach,* and *Ha Mashiach* is "The Anointed One," the Messiah. The Scriptures teach that the Messiah will serve in all three offices: as prophet, priest, and king.

> *I have found My servant David; With My holy oil I have anointed him,*
> *With whom My hand shall be established; Also My arm shall strengthen him.*
>
> —*Psalm 89:20–21 (NKJV)*

Prophet

In ancient Israel, the role of prophets was to make known God's ways to the people. These men and women exhorted the nation to obedience and loyalty, pronounced blessings, and warned of impending disaster. Some performed miracles, and some foretold the coming of the Messiah.

Moses was Israel's most famous prophet, and God promised to send another like him to instruct the people:

> *I will raise up for them a prophet like you from among their brothers.*
> *And I will put my words in his mouth, and he shall speak to them all that I*
> *command him. And whoever will not listen to my words that he shall speak in my*
> *name, I myself will require it of him.*
>
> *—Deuteronomy 18:18–19 (NKJV)*

Isaiah 61:1–2

Centuries later, Isaiah spoke of an anointed prophet who would proclaim a gracious message.

7. *This prophet will announce blessings of:*

   a) _____ *for the afflicted;*

   b) _____ *for broken hearts;*

   c) _____ *for captives;*

   d) _____ *prison doors; and*

   e) _____ *for all who mourn.*

Priest

Psalm 110:1–7

In ancient Egypt, the pharaoh served not only as king but also as high priest, performing the rituals that supposedly kept the cosmos functioning smoothly.[3] By contrast, in ancient Israel, the offices of king and priest were entirely separate. No king presided over sacrifices in the temple, and no priest had authority to govern in the civil realm.

In Psalm 110, however, David spoke of a future king who would also be a priest of the order of Melchizedek (Gen. 14:18).[4]

8. *How long will this future king serve in the office of priest (v. 4)?*

_____

Zechariah 6:11–13

The prophet Zechariah, living in the fifth century B.C., also spoke of a ruler whose throne would unite the offices of king and priest.

9. *What is the name of this man?*

_____

> *Even he shall build the temple of the LORD; and he shall bear the glory, and shall sit and rule upon his throne; and he shall be a priest upon his throne: and the counsel of peace shall be between them both.*
>
> —*Zechariah 6:13 (KJV)*

King

Numerous prophecies in the Bible predict the coming of a "branch," or descendant, of David who will reign on his throne and establish God's kingdom throughout the earth. The examples below provide details about the character, extent, and duration of His reign.

Isaiah 9:6–7
In this prophecy, Isaiah announces the birth of a king who will establish peace and reign on the throne of David forever.

10. *His titles will include:*

a) _____

b) _____

c) _____

d) _____

Isaiah 11:1–12
This prophecy looks forward to a specially anointed king, a descendant of Jesse, the father of King David. The Spirit of *Yahweh* will empower Him with wisdom and understanding, counsel and might, knowledge and the fear of the Lord. Because of His reverence for God, He will not be fooled by appearances or lying words but will judge fairly and with righteousness, and the nations will seek His counsel.

11. *What will He do for His dispersed people (vv. 11–12)?*

_____

_____

During this king's reign, nature will be restored to its pre-Fall harmony, and people and animals will no longer prey upon each other.

> *The wolf shall dwell with the lamb, and the leopard shall lie down with the young goat, and the calf and the lion and the fattened calf together; and a little child shall lead them. They shall not hurt or destroy in all my holy mountain; for the earth shall be full of the knowledge of the LORD as the waters cover the sea.*
>
> *Isaiah 11:6, 9 (ESV)*

Micah 5:2–4

Micah predicts the coming of a king who is "from of old, from ancient days," who will feed His flock (Israel) in the strength and majesty of the name of *Yahweh*.

> *12. How far will His authority extend?*

According to these Scriptures, the Promised One, the Messiah, will be a prophet, a priest, and a king who will reign forever on the throne of David. He will gather and defend God's chosen people, instruct the nations in God's ways, and establish peace in the earth.

What these prophecies do not reveal is how He will defeat the adversary, Satan. This question and others remained a mystery in 740 B.C., when Isaiah began his prophetic ministry in Jerusalem.

The Mission

> *Remember not the former things, nor consider the things of old. Behold, I am doing a new thing; now it springs forth, do you not perceive it? I will make a way in the wilderness and rivers in the desert.*
>
> *—Isaiah 43:18–19 (ESV)*

Through the prophet Isaiah, God provided new details about the Messiah and His mission as Rescuer. Five scripture passages in the book of Isaiah shed light on God's plan for the One He calls "My Servant."

Isaiah 42:1–9

In the first passage, God introduces His Servant: He has chosen Him, upholds and delights in Him, and has anointed Him with His Spirit.

> The term "servant," as opposed to "slave," connotes a contractual relationship freely entered into, such as that between a suzerain and a vassal-king. [5]

13. *This anointed Servant-King is to establish* _____

    in the earth (vv. 1, 4).

The Hebrew word *mishpat* (justice) designates not only judicial decision-making but government in all its processes—judicial, legislative, and executive.[6] God's sovereign authority is the foundation of all government, and the Servant is to establish His will and purposes throughout the earth, revealing truth to the nations.[7]

Then, identifying Himself as the Creator of heaven and earth, God proclaims His plan for His Servant.

14. *God has called the Servant in righteousness and promises to keep Him*

    and give Him as:

    a) _____ *and*

    b) _____ .

The Servant will be a blessing to all peoples, and His mission will create a historical watershed, establishing a new covenant between God and the human race.

> *I am the LORD.*
> *I have called you in righteousness;*
> *I will take you by the hand and keep you;*
> *I will give you as a covenant for the people, a light for the nations,*
> *to open the eyes that are blind, to bring out the prisoners from the dungeon,*
> *from the prison those who sit in darkness.*
> *I am the LORD.*
>
> *—Isaiah 42:6–8a (ESV)*

Mission Accepted

Isaiah 49:5–9a

In the second passage, the Servant affirms His calling and commitment by repeating God's promise that He will not only restore the tribes of Jacob but will also be a light to the nations.

Yet, God cautions His Servant that He will not be universally acclaimed—quite the contrary.

15. *What kind of reception can He expect from His contemporaries (v. 7)?*

_____

_____

16. *Still, at some point, how will the rulers of the earth respond to Him?*

_____

_____

Will these reactions take place simultaneously or at different times? The passage closes without saying, only repeating God's promises to preserve His Servant and to give Him as a covenant so that captives can be set free, dark places enlightened, and desolate territory reclaimed.

Isaiah 50:4–7

The third passage describes how God has prepared the Servant for His mission, speaking to Him morning by morning. The Servant understands that He will suffer rejection, but He is determined to carry out the plan. Trusting in God to help Him, He will submit voluntarily to the physical ordeal that lies ahead.

> In Hebrew, when the past tense describes a future action or event, as in Isaiah 50:6, it emphasizes its certainty. That is, the writer regards it as being so firmly established in the divine will and purpose as to be already a reality. This device is known as the "prophetic perfect." [8]

Isaiah 52:13–15

In the fourth passage, God confirms that His Servant will be not only honored and exalted but horribly abused and disfigured.

This prophecy also provides a clue as to the reason for His suffering.

17. According to verse 15, what will result from the Servant's suffering?

_____

_____

In the Bible, the word "sprinkle" occurs almost exclusively in connection with the blood of sacrificed animals. Priests sprinkled blood to atone for sins, cleanse from disease, and consecrate other priests; at Mount Sinai, blood was sprinkled on the Israelites to ratify the covenant.[9]

What type of sprinkling is to result from the Servant's mission? Will He atone for sins? Cleanse people suffering from diseases? Consecrate priests? Ratify a covenant? The next chapter of Isaiah—the fifth passage—offers some surprisingly clear answers.

> *Rejoice greatly, O daughter of Zion! Shout, O daughter of Jerusalem!*
> *Behold, your King is coming to you; He is just and having salvation,*
> *Lowly and riding on a donkey, A colt, the foal of a donkey.*
>
> *—Zechariah 9:9 (NKJV)*

The Suffering Servant

Isaiah 53:1–4
More clearly than any other passage of Scripture, Isaiah 53 provides details as to how the Servant, acting as *Yahweh's* "arm," or agent, will carry out His priestly mission.

Lacking any vestige of kingly majesty, the "arm of the LORD" will be despised and rejected by men. He will be not only acquainted with grief and sorrows but will take upon Himself the sicknesses and pains of others in order to carry them away.[10]

Isaiah 53:5–9
Some will surmise that the Servant is being punished for His own sins (v. 4).

Cave at Qumran National Park.
© Ella Hanochi/Shutterstock.com

In 1947, Bedouin shepherds discovered seven scrolls in a cave about one mile west of the Dead Sea. The largest and best preserved among them was the Great Isaiah Scroll, containing the entire book of the prophet Isaiah. The scroll dates from about 125 B.C.

18. What will be the actual cause of His wounds?

_____

_____

19. In verse 7, He is compared to:

_____

_____.

Having no guilt of His own, He will be put to death for the transgressions of others.

Isaiah 53:10–12

20. Whose will is it that He be bruised and put to death?

_____

Yet, the Servant will not remain in the grave; He will live, and God's purpose will prosper in His hand. Having allowed Himself to be put to death as an offering, this Kinsman-Redeemer will see and be satisfied with the results of His suffering: many sinners will be "made righteous"—i.e., acquitted of guilt and given right standing with God.

The Servant in the Psalms

Psalms 16, 22, and 40 complement the descriptions of the Servant in the book of Isaiah, shedding additional light on His person and mission. Psalm 98 celebrates the success of the Servant's mission and anticipates the day when He will return to restore and govern the earth.

Psalm 16:8–11
This psalm speaks of God's "holy one," who, in facing death, has a confident, almost joyful tone.

The Great Isaiah Scroll, column 44 (Isaiah 53). Shrine of the Book, © The Israel Museum, Jerusalem, by Ardon Bar-Hama.

21. *He has confidence that God will not:*

a) _____

nor will He b) _____ *;*

instead, He will c) _____ *.*

Psalm 22:1–31

The first part of this psalm is the prayer of a dying man who listens as onlookers taunt Him with the claims He has made about His relationship with God (vv. 7–8). He is aware that others are dividing among themselves the garments they have stripped from Him.

22. *Briefly describe the condition of the Speaker in the following verses:*

(v. 1) _____

(vv. 6–8) _____

(vv. 14–15) _____

(vv. 16–17) _____

(v. 18) _____

Beginning with verse 22, the tone changes abruptly. Instead of rejection and suffering, there is joy and celebration. The Speaker vows to declare God's name to his brothers—His near kinsmen—and praise *Yahweh* in the congregation.

He announces blessings: the poor will eat and be satisfied; those who seek God will find Him; and "hearts" will live forever.[11] All peoples—rich and poor, strong and weak—will worship God and submit to Him as King, and one generation will tell of His righteousness to the next, making known what He has done.[12]

Psalm 40:6–10

These verses speak of a time when animal sacrifices are not required to atone for transgressions. The change seems connected with the coming of One who listens to God, delights to do His will, and has His laws written on His heart.[13]

23. Where is His coming foretold?

_____

24. The Speaker in Psalm 40 also proclaims glad news in the great congregation, declaring God's righteousness in connection with His (v. 10):

a) _____ *and*

b) _____ ;

c) _____ *and*

d) _____ .

> *Mercy and truth are met together; Righteousness and peace have kissed.*
> *Truth shall spring out of the earth, And righteousness shall look down from heaven.*
>
> *—Psalm 85:10 (NKJV)*

A New Song

Psalm 98:1–9

This psalm celebrates the victory won by God's "holy arm": it is His salvation, His righteousness, His mercy and faithfulness that are worthy of praise. He has done the work necessary to set captives free from the curse and open the way for people of all nations to enjoy fellowship with Him forever.

> *Oh, sing to the LORD a new song!*
> *For He has done marvelous things;*
> *His right hand and His holy arm have gained Him the victory.*
>
> *The LORD has made known His salvation;*
> *His righteousness He has revealed in the sight of the nations.*
>
> *He has remembered His mercy and His faithfulness to the house of Israel;*
> *All the ends of the earth have seen the salvation of our God.*
>
> *—Psalm 98:1–3 (NKJV)*

Through the work of the Promised One, God has triumphed over Satan and fulfilled His promises to Adam and Eve, to his chosen people, and to all who put their trust in Him. The concluding verses of this Psalm look forward to His coming reign in righteousness as King over all the earth—just as He has promised.

*Shout joyfully to the L*ORD *all the earth;*
Break forth in song, rejoice, and sing praises.

*Sing to the L*ORD *with the harp,*
With the harp and the sound of a psalm,

With trumpets and the sound of a horn;
*Shout joyfully before the L*ORD*, the King.*

Let the sea roar, and all its fullness,
The world and those who dwell in it;

Let the rivers clap their hands;
*Let the hills be joyful together before the L*ORD*,*

For He is coming to judge the earth.
With righteousness He shall judge the world,
And the peoples with equity.

—Psalm 98:4–9 (NKJV)

Notes:

Epilogue

When Augustus was emperor of Rome and Herod governed the province of Judea, a son was born to an elderly Jewish priest named Zechariah and his wife, Elizabeth. According to custom, the parents arranged for the child to be circumcised on the eighth day, and their relatives and friends gathered together to celebrate the occasion. The Jewish practice of circumcision had originated in the time of Abraham, some 2,000 years ago, and would seal the baby's inclusion in the covenant family of God.

The proud father, Zechariah, had to be content with smiling at his guests rather than conversing with them. He had been mute for nearly a year, ever since his encounter with an angel while on duty in the temple. The angel had announced he would have a son, but Zechariah had doubted the message and consequently lost his ability to speak.

Those present expected the baby to be named for his father or another living relative, as was the custom. However, when the moment arrived to announce his name, Elizabeth declared that he was to be called "John." Her surprised guests objected, noting that no one in their family was called by that name. They motioned to Zechariah: Did he agree? Was this the name he wanted for his child? Zechariah asked for a writing tablet and quickly wrote the name the angel had given him. His son would be called "John."

Immediately, Zechariah's tongue was freed, and he began to glorify God and to prophesy the fulfillment of an ages-old promise: that God would send a Rescuer for all people, a Light to shine in the darkness—the Messiah! Zechariah then foretold his son's mission: when grown, John would go before the Messiah as a prophet and prepare God's people to receive Him.

After the ceremony, the guests continued to discuss the events they had witnessed that day, sharing what they had seen and heard with others, until the Judean hills fairly buzzed with speculation about John's future mission and the coming of the Messiah, the Promised One:

Who would He be?
When and where would He appear?
How could He be recognized?
What would He do?

(Account based on Luke 1:57–80.)

In the fifteenth year of the reign of Tiberius Caesar,...
the word of God came to John the son of Zechariah in the wilderness.
And he went into all the region around the Jordan,
proclaiming a baptism of repentance for the forgiveness of sins.
As it is written in the book of Isaiah the prophet,
The voice of one crying in the wilderness,
"Prepare the way of the Lord, make his paths straight."

—Luke 3:1–4

There was a man sent from God, whose name was John.
He came as a witness, to bear witness about the light,
that all might believe through him.
He was not the light,
but came to bear witness about the light.

—John 1:6–8

The next day he saw Jesus coming toward him, and said,
"Behold, the Lamb of God, who takes away the sin of the world!"
This is he of whom I said, "After me comes a man who ranks before me,
because he was before me."
I myself did not know him, but for this purpose I came baptizing with water,
that he might be revealed to Israel.

—John 1:29–31

Answer Key

Chapter 1: The Promise

1. Various answers: Personality, the ability to think rationally, experience emotions, appreciate beauty, imagine and create objects, communicate in words, think in terms of right and wrong, etc.

2. He gave them dominion over the sea creatures, the birds, and all creatures that move upon the earth.

3. He would die.

4. To keep her from gaining knowledge that would make her "like God."

5. Fear.

6. He blamed Eve.

7. She blamed the serpent.

8. The relationship would be one of enmity.

9. They would have lived forever in their fallen condition.

10. She said she gave birth to Cain "with the help of the Lord."

11. He needed to offer a firstborn of the flock for a sacrifice.

Chapter 2: Abraham

1. Abram had to leave his relatives and depart for a land God would show him.

2. He built an altar and called on the name of the LORD (*YHWH*).

3. He didn't.

4. Various answers: To seek direction as to where in Canaan to settle; to thank God for protecting him and causing him to prosper; to thank God for His promises; to remind God of His promises.

5. By letting Lot choose, Abram trusted God to supply his own needs.

6. God Most High, Possessor of heaven and earth.

7.   The Lord, God Most High, Possessor of heaven and earth.

8.   He repeated His promises to give him a son and many descendants.

9.   He "counted it to him for righteousness."

10. A smoking firepot and a flaming torch (answers will vary).

11. He fell prostrate before God.

12. He promised to multiply his descendants. Ishmael would become the father of twelve princes and would become a great nation.

13. a) A great and powerful nation; b) all the nations of the earth.

14. His justice.

15. He invited Abraham to live wherever he wished in his territory.

16. He said that he and Isaac would come back after the sacrifice.

17. As a "mighty prince."

Chapter 3: Heirs of Promise

1.   The founders of two nations were fighting in her womb.

2.   The younger. God said the older would serve his younger brother.

3.   Isaac was to remain in Gerar and not go to Egypt.

4.   He said that Abraham had obeyed His voice and kept His commands, statutes, and laws (Gen. 26:5).

5.   He built an altar and called on God's name.

6.   He saw that the LORD (*Yahweh*) was with Isaac.

7.   "Let everyone be cursed who curses you."

8.   a) Many descendants; b) the land of Canaan as an inheritance.

9.   That in Jacob's offspring, all nations of the earth would be blessed.

10. He had a reverent fear of and respect for the Almighty.

11. He promised to be "with him."

12. It signified that God would protect Jacob and provide for his needs.

13. To ensure that Jacob would treat his daughters well.

14. He prayed.

15. a) That He would do him good (cause him to prosper); b) that He would make his descendants like the sand of the sea which cannot be numbered for multitude.

16. Surrender all statues and figures of other gods, along with any jewelry associated with them.

17. He caused the Canaanites to fear them.

18. a) Multiply him and make him a company of peoples; b) give the land of Canaan to his descendants as an everlasting possession.

19. He said that Joseph was the one set apart from his brothers.

20. He made them swear an oath.

Chapter 4: Kinsman-Redeemer

1. He feared that, if Egypt were invaded, the Hebrews would rise up and join the attacking forces.

2. The Egyptian people.

3. His covenant with Abraham, Isaac, and Jacob.

4. He identified Himself as "the God of Abraham, Isaac, and Jacob."

5. a) To be with him; b) Moses would return and serve God "on this mountain."

6. He was to say "I AM has sent me to you."

7. He said He would be with Moses' mouth.

8. They bowed their heads and worshiped.

9. He said he didn't "know the Lord."

10. They refused to listen to him.

11. They saw him as "very great in the land of Egypt."

12. He commanded them to sacrifice a lamb or a goat and place the blood on the doorposts of their homes.

13. In the Promised Land.

14. He asked him to pronounce a blessing on him.

15. They feared they all might die if the Hebrews remained in Egypt.

16. The males had to be circumcised.

17. Parents were to redeem their firstborn sons by the sacrifice of a lamb.

18. The vow Joseph's brothers swore to take his bones with them when they left.

19. They panicked, telling Moses they wished they had stayed in Egypt.

20. The pillar of cloud came between them, bringing darkness to the Egyptians and light to the Israelites.

Chapter 5: A Chosen Nation

1. a) Listened to His voice; b) did what was right in His sight; c) obeyed His commandments; and d) kept His statutes.

2. He didn't.

3. The Lord (*Yahweh*).

4. He didn't.

5. He offered a burnt offering and sacrifices.

6. a) God's treasured possession; b) a kingdom of priests; c) a holy nation.

7. 6) You shall protect human life; 7) You shall honor your marriage vows; 8) You shall respect the property of others; 9) You shall speak the truth; 10) You shall love your neighbor as yourself and seek happiness only with your own spouse and your own possessions.

8. Because the Israelites had been strangers in Egypt.

Chapter 6: The Promised Land

1. His sworn promise to Abraham, Isaac, and Israel (Jacob) to multiply their descendants and give them the land of Canaan.

2. He might destroy them before they reached the Promised Land because they were a "stiff-necked people."

3. a) They stood at their tent doors when Moses went to the Tent of Meeting. b) When the pillar of cloud stood at the Tent of Meeting, they stood in their tent doorways and worshiped.

4. They were to be anointed with oil.

5. He was to place his hands on the animal's head before killing it.

6. So that the Israelites would not offer sacrifices to other gods.

Chapter 7: The Promised One

1. a) Judah. b) A King will come from Judah's line whom the peoples will obey.

2. a) Judah (Bethlehem). b) A King will come from Bethlehem to rule in Israel. He is "from of old, from ancient days."

3. a) David. b) God has promised to establish David's offspring and his throne forever.

4. a) David. b) God will raise up a righteous Branch who will reign as king and execute justice and righteousness. He will be called "The LORD is our righteousness."

5. a) The House of David. b) A virgin of the house of David will bear a son and call Him Immanuel.

6. a) God. b) God will give His Son the nations as His inheritance.

7. a) Good news; b) binding up, healing; c) liberty; d) opening; e) comfort.

8. Forever.

9. The Branch.

10. a) Wonderful Counselor; b) Mighty God; c) Everlasting Father; d) Prince of Peace

11. He will recover them from the nations where they have been dispersed.

12. To the ends of the earth.

13. Justice

14. a) A covenant to the people; b) a light to the nations.

15. They will despise and reject Him.

16. They will rise up to honor Him and bow down in submission to Him.

17. He will sprinkle many nations.

18. Our transgressions and iniquities.

19. A lamb being led to the slaughter.

20. God's will.

21. a) Abandon Him to the grave; b) allow His body to see corruption; c) show Him the path of life.

22. (v. 1) Forsaken, suffering; (vv. 6–8) despised, mocked, rejected; (vv. 14–15) weak, thirsty; (vv. 16–17) pierced in hands and feet; (v. 18) stripped of clothing.

23. In the volume of the Book (Scroll).

24. a) Faithfulness; b) salvation; c) steadfast love; d) truth or faithfulness. (Answers may vary, depending on the version of the Bible used.)

Works Cited

Bibles

JPS Hebrew-English Tanakh, Second Edition. Philadelphia: The Jewish Publication Society, 1999.

The Amplified Bible. Grand Rapids: Zondervan Publishing House, 1987.

The English Standard Version Study Bible. Wheaton: Crossway Bibles, 2008.

The Holy Bible, New King James Version. Nashville: Thomas Nelson, Inc., 1982.

The NIV Study Bible, New International Version. General Editor, Kenneth Barker. Grand Rapids: The Zondervan Corporation, 1985.

The Ryrie Study Bible, expanded ed. King James Version. Edited by Charles Caldwell Ryrie. Chicago: Moody Press, 1986, 1994.

1599 Geneva Bible. White Hall, West Virginia: Tolle Lege Press, 2006.

Reference Works

Freedman, David Noel, ed. *The Anchor Bible Dictionary.* New York: Doubleday, 1992.

Gesenius, Wilhelm. Trans. Samuel Prideaux. *Hebrew and Chaldee Lexicon to the Old Testament Scriptures.* Grand Rapids: Baker Book House, 1979.

Harris, R. Laird, Archer L. Gleason, and Bruce K. Waltke. *Theological Wordbook of the Old Testament.* Chicago: The Moody Bible Institute, 1980.

Strong, James. *The New Strong's Exhaustive Concordance of the Bible.* Nashville: Thomas Nelson Publishers, 1984.

Robert Young. *Young's Analytical Concordance.* Hendrickson Publishers Marketing, LLC, 2014.

Books

Arnold, Bill T. and Bryan E. Beyer, eds. *Readings from the Ancient Near East: Primary Sources for Old Testament Study*. Grand Rapids: Baker Academic, 2002.

David, Rosalie. *Cult of the Sun*. London: J.M. Dent & Sons, Ltd., 1980.
-------.*The Ancient Egyptians*. London: Routledge & Kegan Paul, 1982.

Dosick, Wayne. *Living Judaism: The Complete Guide to Jewish Belief, Tradition, and Practice*. HarperSanFrancisco, 1995.

Hillers, Delbert R. *Covenant: The History of a Biblical Idea*. Baltimore: The Johns Hopkins University Press, 1969.

Josephus. *The Works of Josephus,* complete and unabridged. Trans. by William Whiston. Peabody, MA: Hendrickson Publishers, 1987.

Kasdan, Barney. *God's Appointed Customs*. Baltimore: Lederer Books, 1996.
-------*God's Appointed Times*. Lederer Publications, 1993.

Kaster, Joseph. *Wings of the Falcon: Life and Thought in Ancient Egypt*. New York: Holt, Rinehart and Winston, 1968.

Morenz, Siegfried. *Egyptian Religion,* trans. Ann E. Keep. Ithaca: Cornell University Press, 1960, 1973.

Nelson, Ethel R., Richard E. Broadberry, and Ginger Tong Chock. *God's Promise to the Chinese*. Dunlap, TN: Read Books Publishers, 1997.

Redford, Donald B., ed. *The Ancient Gods Speak: A Guide to Egyptian Religion*. New York: Oxford University Press, 2002.

Schaeffer, Francis A. *Genesis in Space and Time*. Downers Grove: InterVarsity Press, 1972.

-------*25 Basic Bible Studies*. Wheaton, IL: Crossway Books, a division of Good News Publishers, 1996.

Skousen, W. Cleon. *The Making of America.* Washington, D.C.: The National Center for Constitutional Studies, 1985.

Walton, John H. *Ancient Near Eastern Thought and the Old Testament.* Grand Rapids, MI: Baker Academic, 2006.

White, Jon Manchip. *Everyday Life in Ancient Egypt.* New York: G.P. Putnam's Sons, 1973.

Wilkinson, Richard H. *The Complete Gods and Goddesses of Ancient Egypt.* London: Thames & Hudson, 2003.

Periodicals

Mendenhall, George E. "Covenant Forms in Israelite Tradition," *The Biblical Archaeologist,* 17:3. Jerusalem and Baghdad: American Schools of Oriental Research, 1954.

Olofsson, Folke T. "The History and Revelation of Anamnesis in Platonic, Jewish, and Christian Thought," *Touchstone* magazine, March/April 2013.

Robinson, Rich. "Jewish Core Values, Part Six," *Jews for Jesus Newsletter,* October 2013.

Websites

Easton, Burton Scott. "Thigh." Bible Study Tools. www.biblestudytools.com/encyclopedias/isbe/thigh.html

Greenberg, Moshe. "Oath in the Bible." American-Israeli Cooperative Enterprise. www.jewishvirtuallibrary.org/jsource/judaica/ejud_0002_0015_0_14994.html

Kohler, Kaufmann. *"Adonai."* The Kopelman Foundation. The Jewish Encyclopedia. www.jewishencyclopedia.com

Endnotes

Chapter 1: The Promise

[1] R. Laird Harris, Gleason L. Archer, Bruce K. Waltke, eds., *Theological Wordbook of the Old Testament* (Chicago: Moody Publishers, 1980), 93. Hereinafter cited as *TWOT*. In the Tenach, or Old Testament, other Scriptures that seem to indicate more than one person in the Godhead include Gen. 3:22; Ps. 2:7; Prov. 8:22–31, 30:4; I Sam. 10:6, 10: 2 Chron. 15:1; Isa. 48:16. The verb in Gen. 1:1 is singular.

[2] The verb *bara'* emphasizes the initiation of an object rather than the shaping of already-existing material and therefore is compatible with the idea of creation *ex nihilo* (*TWOT*, 93). In Egyptian legends, the first gods originated from within primordial matter, as manifestations of a divine energy or essence. The God of Genesis, on the other hand, did not bring forth the heavens and the earth out of already-existing matter or as "an extension of Himself or His essence" (Francis Schaeffer, *25 Basic Bible Studies* [Wheaton, IL: Crossway Books, 1996], 24).

[3] In the ancient world, naming something indicated sovereignty or ownership (*TWOT*, 2063). See also *The Ryrie Study Bible, Expanded Edition,* King James Version, ed. Charles Caldwell Ryrie (Chicago: Moody Publishers, 1994), note on Gen. 1:10 (hereinafter cited as *RyrieSB*); and *The NIV Study Bible,* ed. Ken Barker (Grand Rapids: The Zondervan Corporation, 1985), note on Gen. 1:5 (hereinafter cited as *NIVSB*).

[4] *TWOT*, 278; Francis Schaeffer, *Genesis in Space and Time* (Downers Grove: Intervarsity Press, 1972), 33.

[5] *Strong's,* 7673; *TWOT*, 2323. The *1599 Geneva Bible* comments that God rested "from creating his creatures, but not from governing and preserving them." (White Hall, West Virginia: Tolle Lege Press, 2006, note on Ex. 31:17.)

[6] *TWOT*, 25a and 25b.

[7] The ancient Chinese used pictographs to record a creation account which has striking parallels to the Genesis account. Some pictographs may hold a clue as to why, before the Fall, Adam and Eve were not embarrassed by their nakedness. A graph that means "light," "glorious," or "naked" shows a kneeling man and woman who are both "covered" by the symbol for fire. (Ethel R. Nelson, Richard E. Broadberry, and Ginger Tong Chock, *God's Promise to the Chinese* [Dunlap, TN: Read Books Publisher, 1997], 26, 29.) Psalm 104:1–2 describes God as covered with light "as with a garment" (ESV); the JPS says He is "clothed in glory and majesty, wrapped in a robe of light."

[8] Genesis 3:16 is often interpreted as being *prescriptive*, i.e., requiring Eve to submit to Adam as ruler. However, many understand the language as *descriptive*, i.e., indicating how the original, complementary roles of husband and wife will be distorted. See *The English Standard Version Study Bible* (Wheaton: Crossway Bibles, a publishing ministry of Good News Publishers, 2008), note on Gen. 3:16. Hereinafter cited as *ESVSB*.

[9] The ancient Chinese character for "righteousness" shows a "sheep" covering the character for "me," which is composed of the symbols for "hand" and "lance." (*See* Nelson, Broadberry, and Chock, *God's Promise to the Chinese*, pp. 26, 29. The pictographs are reproduced by permission.) The modern (traditional) Chinese character for "righteousness" retains this symbolism.

<u>Ancient Character</u>   <u>Traditional Character</u>

hand + lance = me + sheep = righteousness

Chapter 2: Abraham

[1] In the biblical worldview, the universe is an "open" system: God exists independently of His creation and continues to act into it, and He is all-powerful. In the ancient Near Eastern worldview, the universe was a "closed" system: the gods operated only within the cosmos; they did not transcend it, and none was all-powerful (John H. Walton, *Ancient Near Eastern Thought and the Old Testament* [Grand Rapids: Baker Academic, 2006], 97–99, 103. Hereinafter cited as *ANET*).

[2] More than fifty treaties dating from the second millennium B.C. have been discovered; most are suzerainty treaties from the ancient Hittite empire (1425–1180 B.C.), including one that defines the relationship between a Hittite ruler and the Egyptian pharaoh Rameses II. (Ibid., 69; David Noel Freedman, ed., *The Anchor Bible Dictionary* [New York: Doubleday, 1992], s.v. "Covenant." Hereinafter cited as *ABD*.)

For more information on suzerainty treaties, see George E. Mendenhall, "Covenant Forms in Israelite Tradition," in *The Biblical Archaeologist*, ed. G. Ernest Wright and Frank M. Cross, Jr., with the assistance of Floyd V. Filson in New Testament matters (Jerusalem and Baghdad: American Schools of Oriental Research, 1954), 17, 3:56–61. See also Bill T. Arnold and Bryan E. Beyer, eds. *Readings from the Ancient Near East* (Grand Rapids: Baker Academic, 2002), 96–103.

[3] Delbert Hillers, *Covenant: The History of a Biblical Idea* (Baltimore: The Johns Hopkins University Press, 1969), 152–54. Hereinafter cited as *Covenant*. See also *ABD*, s.v. "Treaties in the ANE."

In Malachi 1:6, God uses these terms in reference to His relationship with Israel: "A son honors his father, and a servant his master. If then I am a father, where is my honor? And if I am a master, where is my fear? says the LORD of hosts to you, O priests, who despise my name" (ESV).

[4] God had told Abram to separate himself from his relatives in Haran (Gen. 12:1). Abram's decision to let Lot accompany him was to have far-reaching consequences. Lot's grandsons Moab and Ammon founded nations that became enemies of Israel (Gen. 19:30–38; Num. 22–24; Judg. 10:6–18).

[5] Some versions, including the KJV, NKVJ, ESV, and NIV, put "Lord" in small capital letters when it means *Yahweh*, to distinguish it from *Adonai*, also translated as "Lord." The

name *Yahweh* emphasizes God's self-existing nature; the title *Adonai* indicates sovereignty (*Strong's* 3068, 113, 136; *TWOT*, 27b).

6 See *TWOT*, 300; *The New Strong's Exhaustive Concordance of the Bible* (Nashville: Thomas Nelson Publishers, 1984), 1350. Hereinafter cited as *Strong's*. All numerical references for *Strong's* are to the accompanying *Dictionary of the Hebrew Bible (Hebrew and Chaldee Dictionary)*.

7 *Melchizedek* may mean "my king is righteous" (*TWOT*, 1199i) or "king of right" (*Strong's*, 4442). Gesenius translates it as "king of righteousness" (*Gesenius' Hebrew and Chaldee Lexicon*, trans. Samuel Prideaux Tregelles [Grand Rapids: Baker Book House, 1979], 4442. Hereinafter cited as *Gesenius*).

8 The Bible doesn't say what god(s) King Bera worshiped, but throughout the ancient Near East, it was common practice for kings to claim they had been chosen by their gods to rule a specific territory. Hammurapi, in the prologue to his code of laws, claimed that the sun god and the god of storms had chosen him to rule (*ABD*, s.v. "Canaan, Religion of," "Covenant," and "Hittite Religion"; Walton, *ANET*, 137–38; 278–83). If a king offended his god(s), he would lose their favor and protection, leaving his kingdom vulnerable (*see* Walton, *ANET*, 108).

9 Only a king equal in power to the gift-giver could accept a gift without becoming indebted to him (Mendenhall, "Covenant Forms," 58; *ABD*, s.v. "Treaties in the ANE").

10 The Hebrew word *magen* (shield) indicates a small shield carried by soldiers, but it may also signify "suzerain" or "benefactor" (*TWOT*, 367c; *Strong's*, 4043).

11 *Adonai* (my Lord), in a special plural form, is used only to refer to God (*Strong's*, 136; *TWOT*, 27b).

12 The Hebrew for "reward" is *sakar*, meaning "hire," or "wages" (*TWOT*, 2264). *Strong's* defines it as "*payment* of contract," implying *compensation* or *benefit* (7939).

13 The Hebrew word translated "believed" is *'aman. "* It connotes firmness or certainty (*TWOT*, 116).

14 Barney Kasdan, *God's Appointed Customs* (Baltimore: Lederer Books, 1996), 50–52. If a betrothed couple chose not to marry, divorce proceedings were in order. See also Rabbi Wayne Dosick, *Living Judaism* (HarperSanFrancisco, 1995), 296.

15 The Hebrew for this phrase is *karath beriyth*. (*Strong's*, 3772 and 1285; *TWOT*, 1048 and 282a). Other common idioms for a treaty enactment were "to cut an oath" and "treaty and oath" (*ABD*, s.v. "Covenant" and "Treaties in the ANE"; Hillers, *Covenant*, 40–41).

16 The verb in Gen. 15:17 is singular.

17 *NIVSB* note on Gen. 17:5; *Strong's*, 85.

18 *ABD*, s.v. "Covenant."

19 See *NIVSB* note on Gen. 17:10.

20 *Strong's*, 8282 (*sarah*) and 8297 (*sarai*). The root of both words is *sar* (8269), indicating one having authority or dominion over others. Elsewhere in the Old Testament, *sarah* is used to designate noble ladies of the royal court (*TWOT*, 2295b).

21 *RyrieSB* note on Gen. 17:21. See also Arnold and Beyer, *Readings from the Ancient Near East*, 108.

22 *RyrieSB* note on Gen. 20:16.

23 Nonaggression treaties were considered binding upon successors (*ABD*, s.v. "Treaties in the ANE").

24 "Only" (Hebrew, *yachiyd*) derives from a root word meaning "to be one" and may also connote "unique" and "beloved" (*Strong's*, 3173, 3161; *TWOT*, 858).

25 *ABD,* s.v. "Covenant"; Hillers, *Covenant:* 29–38; Mendenhall, "Covenant Forms," 59–61.

Chapter 3: Heirs of Promise

1 See *NIVSB* notes on Gen. 25:5 and 25:23.

2 This king may have been a descendant of the ruler who made a treaty with Abraham (see *NIVSB* notes on Gen. 21:22 and Gen. 26:1).

3 Abimelech acknowledged the God of Isaac by His name *Yahweh* (*YHWH*), translated here as "Lord."

4 Dosick, *Living Judaism*, 298.

5 See *The Amplified Bible, Expanded Edition,* note on Gen. 31:30 (Grand Rapids: Zondervan Bible Publishers and the Lockman Foundation, 1987). Hereinafter cited as AMP.

6 Among modern Bedouin tribes also, one way to make a league is for prospective partners to share a ceremonial feast (Hillers, *Covenant*, 57; see also *ABD*, s.v. "Covenant" and "Treaties in the ANE").

7 The word "man" (Hebrew, *'ish*) in Gen. 32:24–25 connotes a male individual (*Strong's*, 376, *TWOT*, 83a). "Angel" means "messenger," or "representative" (*Strong's* 4397; *TWOT*, 1068a). "Angel" is capitalized because Jacob acknowledged the Angel was God (Genesis 31:30). *See* Genesis 31:11–13 and Genesis 48:16.

8 *Strong's,* 3409; *TWOT*, 916a. *See* Moshe Greenberg, "Oath in the Bible," American-Israeli Cooperative Enterprise, www.jewishvirtuallibrary.org. This article cites Gen. Raba, quoted by Rashi. *See also* Burton Scott Easton, www.biblestudytools.com/encyclopedias/isbe/thigh. html). Some scholars view the Angel's gesture as a reference to the life-force.

In Exodus 1:5, the KJV speaks of Jacob's descendants as "all the souls who came out of the loins of Jacob." The Hebrew word translated "loins" in this verse (*yarek*) also means "thigh" (*TWOT*, 916a).

9 *Strong's,* 3290.

10 *TWOT*, 2287. *Strong's* translates it as "he will rule as God" (3478). The root words are the verb *sarah* (8280), meaning "to *prevail*—have power (as a prince)," and *el* (410), meaning "strength" or "God."

[11] See *NIVSB* note on Gen. 33:3. Jacob's seven deep bows were a sign of complete submission. When he and Esau met, Jacob addressed Esau as "my lord" and spoke of himself as "his servant" (Gen. 33:14)

[12] *ESVSB*, note on Gen. 33:20. *Strong's* translates it as "the *mighty God of Jisrael*" (415). Shechem was where Abram had first erected an altar when he arrived in Canaan (Gen. 12:6–7).

[13] The meaning of *El Shaddai* is uncertain. Translating it as "God Almighty" dates at least to the third century B.C., when the Hebrew scriptures were translated into Greek. Other possible translations are "the one who is (self-)sufficient" and "God of the mountain" (*TWOT*, 2333); *see also* "Jewish Concepts: the Name of God," www.jewishvirtuallibrary.com.

[14] See *RyrieSB* and *NIVSB* notes on Gen. 48:5.

Chapter 4: Kinsman-Redeemer

[1] According to the first-century Jewish historian Flavius Josephus, an Egyptian scribe prophesied the birth of a Hebrew baby who would one day "bring low" Egypt's dominion, and his prophecy resulted in pharaoh's order to destroy the Hebrew male infants. ("The Antiquities of the Jews," bk. 2:9.2 in *The Works of Josephus: New Updated Edition* [Peabody, MA: Hendrickson Publishers, 1987], trans. by William Whiston. Hereinafter cited as "Antiquities.")

[2] Ibid., bk. 2:10.

[3] Josephus identified Midian as a city that "lay upon the Red Sea" (ibid., bk. 2:11.1). The apostle Paul locates Midian in Arabia (Gal. 4:25).

[4] To forget a covenant was to break it (*ABD*, s.v. "Treaties in the ANE"). The Hebrew verb *zakar* here implies not only recalling but also taking appropriate action (*TWOT*, 551; *ABD*, s.v. "Covenant").

[5] *Strong's*, 3068, 136; *RyrieSB* and *NIVSB* notes on Exodus 3:14. The four letters in Hebrew are known as "the tetragrammaton."

[6] God's name *Yahweh* (I AM) would challenge the Egyptian view of the universe as a closed, pantheistic system: Egyptian gods did not exist independently of the universe and none was all-powerful (*see* Walton, *ANET*, 97–99, 103, 199).

[7] Rosalie David, *Cult of the Sun* (London: J.M. Dent & Sons, Ltd., 1980), 93. Scholars debate the identity of the pharaoh who reigned during the plagues and the Exodus. Rameses II (1279–1213 B.C.) is one candidate; others include Thutmose II (1493–1479 B.C.), Thutmose III (1479–1425 B.C.), and Amenhotep II (1427–1401 B.C.).

[8] Jon Manchip White, *Everyday Life in Ancient Egypt* (New York: G.P. Putnam's Sons, 1980; text originally published in 1963), 130.

[9] Most English Bibles read "I am the LORD." The practice of substituting "Lord" or *"Adonai"* for the Hebrew *YHWH* (*Yahweh*) became common about the third century B.C., when Jewish

leaders feared that overuse of God's name might violate the third commandment (*TWOT,* 484a; Kaufman Kohler, *"Adonai,"* The Kopelman Foundation, www.jewishencyclopedia.com; *RyrieSB* note on Ex. 3:15).

¹⁰ Joseph Kaster, *Wings of the Falcon: Life and Thought in Ancient Egypt* (New York: Holt, Rinehart and Winston, 1968), 115.

¹¹ Walton, *ANET,* 87–88, 97–99, 184–86; Donald B. Redford, ed., *The Ancient Gods Speak* (New York: Oxford University Press, 3002), 189.

¹² Walton, *ANET,* 278–79; 283; David, *Cult of the Sun,* 85-86; Redford, *The Ancient Gods Speak,* 189. "Both the monarch's legitimization and the efficacy of his reign were ultimately based upon the degree to which he upheld maat, and it was common therefore for kings to style themselves 'beloved of Maat.' (Richard Wilkinson, *The Complete Gods and Goddesses of Ancient Egypt* [New York: Thames & Hudson, 2003], 150. Hereinafter cited as *Complete Gods and Goddesses.*)

¹³ Walton, *ANET,* 152–54; 214–15; Redford, *The Ancient Gods Speak,* 189.

¹⁴ *ABD,* "Egypt, Plagues in"; Walton, *ANET,* 130; Redford, *The Ancient Gods Speak,* 189. Murals on temple walls depicted the king performing priestly rituals (Rosalie David, *The Ancient Egyptians* [London: Routledge & Kegan Paul, 1982], 133–34; *Cult of the Sun,* 73).

¹⁵ The royal *ka,* or divine essence, was believed to unite with the king during his coronation (Redford, *The Ancient Gods Speak,* 68; Wilkinson, *Complete Gods and Goddesses,* 62).

¹⁶ For ancient Near Eastern concepts of creation, the cosmos, the gods, and the origin and purpose of human beings, *see* Walton, *ANET,* 87–99, 147–61, 184–86, 214–15.

¹⁷ *RyrieSB* note on Ex. 7:14–12:36.

¹⁸ Mordechai Becher, *Gateway to Judaism* (Shaara Press, 2005), 46.

¹⁹ In several places, the Bible likens God's relationship with Israel to a marriage. In Hosea 2:19–20, God speaks of betrothing Israel to Himself; and in Jeremiah 31:32 He speaks of Himself as the "husband" of the Israelites: "[Not] like the covenant that I made with their fathers on the day when I took them by the hand to bring them out of the land of Egypt, my covenant that they broke, though I was their husband, declares the Lord" (ESV).

²⁰ According to Exodus 12:37, the men alone numbered approximately 600,000. Adding an equal number of women alone would bring the total to 1.2 million, not counting children.

²¹ The Bible uses military terms to describe the well-organized manner in which the Israelites departed. The NIV says that they were "armed for battle" (Ex. 13:18), and that "the Lord brought the Israelites out of Egypt by their divisions" (Ex. 12:51). *The Amplified Bible* says that they went up "marshaled [in ranks] ..." (Ex. 13:18).

²² Josephus, "Antiquities," bk. 2:15.3. Josephus estimated Pharaoh's army at 600 chariots, 50,000 horsemen and 200,000 foot soldiers (ibid.).

Chapter 5: A Chosen Nation

[1] When the Israelites entered the Promised Land, Jethro's descendants settled with them in the Negev within the territory belonging to Judah (Judg. 1:16).

[2] W. Cleon Skousen, *The Making of America* (Washington, D.C.: The National Center for Constitutional Studies, 1985), 50.

[3] *ABD*, s.v. "Hittite Religion"; David, *Cult of the* Sun, 73–74.

[4] The "Ten Commandments" are not commands but descriptions of expected behavior (*ABD*, s.v. "Covenant"). However, they have the effect of commandments because they are God-given; not to keep them would be an offense against Him. By contrast, in the ancient Near East offenses were seen as sins against the social order rather than against the gods. *See* Walton, *ANET*, 154–55.

[5] Worship of other gods in addition to *Yahweh* would compromise the Israelites' witness that *Yahweh* was distinct in His nature and character from the gods of the Canaanites and other ancient Near Eastern cultures.

Because ancient Canaanite, Mesopotamian, Egyptian, and Greco-Roman cultures shared similar ideas about the nature of the gods and their functions, a god of one culture was sometimes also acknowledged in another. The Canaanite storm-god, *Ba'al,* for example, was at one time also revered in Egypt; and the Egyptian god Amun-Re, who was believed to permeate the entire cosmos, existing in all things, was later equated with the Greek god Zeus (Wilkinson, *Complete Gods and Goddesses,* 94).

[6] *ABD*, s.v. "Hittite Political Structure and Religion"; Siegfried Morenz, *Egyptian Religion,* trans. Ann E. Keep (Ithaca: Cornell University Press, 1960, 1973), 88. Deuteronomy 4:15–20 repeats God's admonition that His people were to make no images.

[7] Walton, *ANET,* 156.

[8] Rich Robinson, "Jewish Core Values, Part Six," *Jews for Jesus Newsletter,* October 2013.

[9] Walton, *ANET,* 157.

[10] The Hebrew word translated "murder" in Exodus 20:13 includes unpremeditated and accidental killing (*TWOT*, 2208). However, God instructed the Israelites to designate "cities of refuge" to which those who unintentionally killed someone could flee for safety from an avenger (Ex. 21:12–14; Num. 35:22–28).

[11] Canaanite culture tolerated adultery, incest, homosexuality, and bestiality. Religious rites involved prostitutes and sometimes child sacrifice. The Ammonites sacrificed children to their god Molech (Lev. 18:21 and 20:2–5; 2 Kings 23:10; Jer. 7:31 and 32:35).

The premise that the natural world is normal—i.e., not fallen from its original state as described in Genesis—can lead to the conclusion that "whatever is, is right."

[12] The sprinkled blood signified a curse: the Israelites acknowledged that they would deserve to die—i.e., become like the sacrificed animals—if they broke the terms of the covenant (*ABD*, s.v. "Covenant").

13 Written treaties of the Late Bronze Age also typically included a list of the gods invoked as witnesses of the pact and called for periodic public reading of the terms (ibid; Mendenhall, "Covenant Forms," 3:58–61).

14 Walton, *ANET*, 143–45.

15 The laws and ordinances given to Moses came to be known as the *Torah,* meaning "teaching." Later, the *Torah* referred to the first five books of the Bible, commonly called "the books of Moses" or "the Law of Moses" (*TWOT*, 910d). After the death of Joshua, the Law was not faithfully taught, and the Bible says that everyone "did what was right in his own eyes" (Josh. 2:10; Judg. 17:6; 21:25).

Chapter 6: Land of Promise

1 According to Deuteronomy 9:18 and 9:25, Moses "lay prostrate before the LORD" for forty days and nights, interceding with God not to destroy the Israelites.

2 "Merciful" (Hebrew, *rahum*) means "compassionate" (*Strong's,* 7349; *TWOT,* 2146c); the Hebrew word "gracious" (*hannun*) occurs only in references to God (*Strong's,* 2587; *TWOT,* 694d). In Ex. 4:22–23, God speaks of Israel as His "son."

3 Three sacrifices called for the death of an animal as a substitute: the burnt offering (Lev. 1:1–17; 6:8–13), the sin offering (Lev. 4:1–5:13), and the guilt offering (Lev. 5:14–6:7).

4 *Strong's,* 3722; *TWOT,* 1023.

Chapter 7: The Promised One

1 The Hebrew word *zera'* (seed, offspring) can denote either an entire line of descendants or one person as representative of them (*TWOT,* 278a).

2 See Ex. 29:7–9; Num. 35:25; I Sam. 9:16, 10:1; Psa.89:20; and I Kings 19:16. In Micah 3:9–12, all three offices are cited. In Ezekiel 22:25–28, God condemns Israel's leaders for unfaithfulness in each of these callings.

3 Walton, *ANET*, 117, 130.

4 Melchizedek was the ancient priest-king to whom Abram once paid tithes. The eternal nature of the order of Melchizedek sets it apart from the later priestly order of Aaron.

5 *Strong's,* 5350; *TWOT,* 1553a. The Bible repeatedly speaks of Moses, Abraham, Jacob, David, the Israelites, and other individuals as "God's servants." *See* Psa. 105:6, 143:12, Isa. 44:1; Jer. 33:22, 26.

6 *Strong's,* 4941; *TWOT,* 2443.

7 Most English translations of Isaiah 42:3 place no commas after "reed" and "wick," making these words direct objects of the verbs "break" and "quench," respectively. The verse indicates

that the Servant will treat the weak with gentleness. In a note, the *JPS Hebrew-English Tanakh* offers an alternate reading by placing commas after "reed" and "wick": "A bruised reed, he shall not be broken; / A dim wick, he shall not be snuffed out." "Reed" and "wick" are then appositives for "Servant," and the verse indicates that the Servant will be bruised but will succeed in His mission.

8   See Nahum Sarna, *Exodus: The Traditional Hebrew Text with the New JPS Translation* (Philadelphia: Jewish Publication Society, 1991), 59.

9   Examples include Leviticus 16:14–19 (atonement for sin); Leviticus 14:1–7 (cleansing from disease); and Exodus 24:5–8 (solemnizing an agreement). In addition, priests and the temple furniture were set apart, or consecrated, by being sprinkled with the blood of sacrificed animals (Ex. 29:19–21; Lev. 8:30) and with the anointing oil (Lev. 40:9–15).

10   In Isaiah 53: 4, "griefs" (Hebrew, *choliy*) is literally "sicknesses" (*TWOT*, 655a). "Sorrows" (Hebrew, *makob*) indicates grief, affliction, and pain (*TWOT*, 940b). The image conveyed is that of a servant taking up a burden in order to carry it away (see *TWOT*, 1421 and 1458).

11   "Heart" refers to the inner or immaterial part of a human being (*TWOT*, 1071b).

12   Most translations of Psalm 22:31 add the word "it" or "this" after "done" (he has done *it*), but no pronoun is in the original Hebrew. The JPS reads "He has acted." The *1599 Geneva Bible* note on this verse says "God hath fulfilled His promise."

13   The Hebrew word for "open" in verse 6 generally means "to bore" and comes from a root meaning "to dig" (*Strong's,* 3738); the NIV translates it "pierced." "Open ear" may refer to openness to God's instructions or to an ear that a servant has allowed to be pierced as a sign of lifelong commitment to a master. (See *NIVSB* note on Psalm 40:6.)

About the Author

A retired college professor, Sally Berk holds a master's degree in English literature from Northwestern University. She has read and studied the Bible for more than forty years and taught about its influence in Western thought and culture. The mother of two adult daughters, Sally lives with her husband, John, in South Carolina. She can be reached at lifespringspress@gmail.com.

Made in the USA
San Bernardino, CA
16 April 2017